LOGIC PRO FOR RECORDING ENGINEERS AND PRODUCERS

quick PRO guides

Logic Pro for Recording Engineers and Producers

Dot Bustelo

Hal Leonard Books
An Imprint of Hal Leonard Corporation

Published in 2012 by Hal Leonard Books
An Imprint of Hal Leonard Corporation
7777 West Bluemound Road
Milwaukee, WI 53213

Trade Book Division Editorial Offices
33 Plymouth St., Montclair, NJ 07042

Printed in the United States of America

Book design by Adam Fulrath
Book composition by Kristina Rolander

Library of Congress Cataloging-in-Publication Data is available upon request.

ISBN 978-1-48541-420-5

www.halleonardbooks.com

CONTENTS

PART II: THE ANATOMY OF EDITING IN LOGIC

Chapter 3

PART III: MIXING IN LOGIC

Chapter 7

Everything About the Mixer 75

Chapter 8

Chapter 9

PART IV: OTHER BASIC STUFF FOR PROS

Chapter 10

PREFACE

When Apple purchased Emagic, my world as an Emagic rep changed dramatically. I was promoted from demonstrating at countless music stores and trade shows for a small German music software and hardware company unknown to the world outside musicians to representing the Worldwide Product Marketing team at Apple, arguably the No. 1 brand in the world. It was an honor now visiting the top studios in the country, the soundchecks and homes of some of the greatest recording artists, producers, and engineers of our time on behalf of Apple, and being able to offer vital technical assistance to their creative workflow.

The tipping point of widespread acceptance was soon crossed for Logic. The interface improved under Apple's guidance, and Logic steadily became more powerful, intuitive, and accessible—which translated to being more credible. No longer did I walk into a studio, let alone a music store, and have to defend Logic or why someone should even look at it. Suddenly, I'd walk into a room and people in high music places who wanted to learn as much as possible about Logic—producers, musicians, and even engineers—were waiting for me! As my good friend, engineer Mark "Exit" Goodchild (who at the time worked for Akon) said, "All the producers I work for use Logic, and I need to know more than them about it so the session can go smoothly." A forward-thinking perspective for the modern engineer accustomed to a Pro Tools–dominated studio environment.

This was the beginning of the new era for Logic where I was welcomed into the studios of the top recording engineers of our times. Their journey into Logic has now become my humble mission to help others navigate. To these engineers, I say thank you for sharing all your questions and gripes over the years. Hopefully the answers are reflected in the chapters that follow and will inspire not just those with your level of technical expertise but also others tasked with going beyond starting a creative idea to realizing their music in Logic.

ACKNOWLEDGMENTS

To my Emagic and Apple family who have freely shared their knowledge and their passion for Logic with me and with so many others through the years. Our process of discovery of the intended and unintentional uses of every new feature in each new version of Logic remain some of my most treasured memories in life. May the spirit of Emagic live on.

With equal gratitude to the countless producers and engineers whose desire for a mastery of Logic and an impatience with it has driven me further into an exploration of Logic's technical potential than I could have imagined I'd go. Especially to the engineers and studios who directly helped with this book on such short notice, especially Phil Tan, Mark "Exit" Goodchild, Jeff Allison, and Alex Lowe, and the special cameo appearances by Bill Lee, Chris "Stone" Garrett, Rick Sheppard, and Greg Kurstin. Always my gratitude to Chad Hugo, Ronnie Vannucci, Empress, Nat Motte, Ryan Tedder, and James Valentine for timeless inspiration. To Brian Miller for his encyclopedic knowledge of Logic. The depth of all of your vision and focus has been daily inspiration, your friendship my honor and privilege. And to the support of three exceptional Atlanta facilities without which this book would not have been written: Atlanta Pro Audio, Milk Money Consulting, and the Ninja Beat Club.

To my family for all their love and support, and to my book editor, Bill Gibson, for making this book possible. To my singer, my music partner, and my muse, Cica, and to our music Perfect Project that would not exist without Logic and that I would not exist without.

To the continued evolution of music through new technology. May it continue to inspire all of us to express the rhythm and the soul of life in new ways.

Logic Pro for Recording Engineers and Producers

quick**PRO**
guides

INTRODUCTION

This book is based on one of the most challenging aspects of my work at Apple, and before that at Emagic—helping professional recording engineers, essentially Pro Tools engineers, work in Logic. I toyed with the idea of naming this book simply *Logic for Pro Tools Users*, which may have sold more copies, but ultimately would have narrowed its audience. Let me explain why.

The first book in this Quick Pro series, *The Power in Logic Pro*, was focused on the creative process in Logic. The goal was to get musicians past the hurdle of learning Logic that I'm happy to have helped so many jump over quickly during the many years I spent on the Apple Logic team. Being a keyboard player and producer myself, I had a natural connection to that discovery process. The very essence of Logic is after all its brilliant design for the music creator.

That book was fun to write. This book also has its share of fun facts to know and tell about Logic, but it is more necessary than fun to write. As more and more musicians use Logic to create music, there are two growing yet divergent sets of users who are engineering in Logic: first, professional engineers whose clients want the Logic workflow maintained, and second, musicians who find themselves engineering their own music. Logic allows them to do so, and besides, there is no alternative for them to realize their music on a small budget.

Let's start with the first group—the professional engineers coming over to Logic. They are generally not switching, but adding Logic to their arsenal and becoming bilingual. Many Logic-based bands and producers today insist that their engineer mix in Logic so that they have access to the finished project for any modifications down the road—whether in length, arrangement, or instrumentation for a radio, video, or live mix, or if they just decide to make a creative change.

The reality is that while Logic may not be the first choice of most professional engineers (there are exceptions), it offers a complete engineering workflow with tools that professional engineers have admitted to me that they appreciate once they discover. For example, there is the ingenious dual channel strip in the Arrange window, allowing the active track and main outs to remain in view. Double whammy—the automatic channel strip creation of an aux track when a plug-in is inserted on a send of the active track.

Then there is that second group of Logic users, who may or may not have any engineering background yet find themselves in a position to record and mix their own music. It makes good sense, both budget-wise and time-wise. The digital mixing tools have become so accessible in Logic that musicians have been empowered to be their own engineer. There are musicians such as the very talented producer Greg Kurstin, who began his career as a jazz keyboard player and guitarist for the likes of Beck, and then went on to produce many hit records that he engineers himself entirely in Logic. How? Greg says he watches professional engineers at every opportunity, then back in his own studio "turns knobs, presses buttons, and uses his ears until it sounds good"—in other words, he experiments intuitively in Logic. Not original, but certainly a tried and true path to creative and scientific success. This second group of the Logic musician-turned-engineer generally does not have the full engineering vocabulary of the professional engineer. This book will hopefully help these readers discover some of that essential terminology—whether solo safe or the default Pan Law.

Learning to engineer is beyond the scope of this book, but hopefully, understanding the Logic tools of the trade will dramatically improve your results. These tools have been specifically refined to help the musician who makes the effort to understand them and to create quality recordings and mixes. There is Logic's brilliant library of settings with crafted channel strip settings containing plug-in chains of reverbs, compressors, and EQs for the task of mixing everything from a bass guitar to a violin to a drum kit—all created by professional engineers and sound designers. Even our friend Greg Kurstin swears by one of the factory mastering channel strip settings on his main outs for many hit records that he has mixed himself.

My advice in *The Power in Logic Pro* was to treat Logic like an instrument, like learning to play the piano or the guitar. I have always reminded new Logic users that you have to learn the language of the instrument, and you have to practice. Take the pressure off yourself of having to create a masterpiece each time you launch the app. You don't even have to feel inspired when you boot it up. You should give yourself focused, disciplined time—besides the time you plan to work in Logic—to learn your instrument.

The challenge with this book for professional engineers needing to learn Logic is that they have little (or believe they have little) time to learn or practice, which translates to the same mental block and stress. Engineers will need to hit the ground running in Logic and work as quickly as they do otherwise to keep up their client workload. If you are a professional engineer taking on a Logic workflow project by necessity, it can certainly be hard to justify "practice time" in Logic.

My response is that I will do my best to make this book concise in order to respect your time constraints and level of annoyance, conscious or unconscious, with the task at hand of learning Logic. I'm confident that as soon as you fully embrace the idea of learning Logic, the Logic Pro that is available today will become satisfying to work with, even as an engineer.

While raw, unadulterated experimentation may work for creating plug-in settings, there are terminology and techniques to grasp that will make your recording, editing, and mixing faster and will help you to achieve results that are more satisfying, musically speaking. Time does need to be spent absorbing and practicing Logic's tools and navigation. Above all, study the key commands to learn the language of Logic. Print them out. Use the trick Copy Key Commands to Clipboard (in the Key Commands window under Options), and then drop them into MS Word to print. In addition to the hot list of my personal favorite 30 key commands shared in appendix A, this book includes another set of invaluable key commands: those that mirror the common keystrokes in Pro Tools. Appendix B gives you nomenclature in Logic that is closely equivalent to the Pro Tools language.

I have a few special introductions. I had the good fortune to bounce ideas for this book off of a few extreme power Logic user friends and convinced them to share some of their favorite techniques with us. I'd like to introduce my longtime partner on the Apple Logic team, the very talented producer and engineer Bill Lee; Rick Sheppard, who recorded and mixed in Logic for the likes of Pink, Gwen Stefani, TLC, and Janet Jackson; and Chris "Stone" Garrett, who has focused his Logic talents as an engineer and programmer for Thievery Corporation. Musician/producer Greg Kurstin, introduced above, also shares a few of his discoveries about Logic engineering on hit records.

As always, it's my pleasure and honor to pass along this body of technical knowledge that was shared with me by the incredibly passionate team of Logic developers and other former colleagues at Apple and Emagic, all of whom I genuinely consider my family.

Methodology of this Book

The topics are loosely grouped into three parts: recording, editing, and then mixing. Though the chapters are logically sequenced to read in a linear fashion, the information in each is self-contained and can be read on its own. Basic navigation of the Logic interface is summarized in the beginning of part 1, "Professional Recording in Logic," and moves rather quickly. These topics were covered in more detail in my previous book, *The Power in Logic Pro*.

Likely a popular section of this book will be the two appendixes mentioned in the Preface, both of which have been directly requested of me by professional recording engineers and producers. Appendix A is my personal favorite "must have" 30 key commands for my own basic driving. Appendix B is a more comprehensive list of terminology and key command equivalents for Pro Tools users. Refer to these documents while going through the book, mark them up with your own notes so these become your go-to "cheat sheets" as you build your momentum in Logic.

There are also QuickTime movies on the accompanying DVD to further illustrate points in the book. I encourage you to watch these so you can see the tools and tricks in action. You should follow along and make time to record, edit, and mix as many projects as possible using the tools in the coming days.

Finally, leave this book somewhere handy in your studio or otherwise nearby to glance back through from time to time. It's amazing how much more of the fine print you can absorb from a book about a feature, after you have begun using it. It's the little things that all add up to what should be a constantly improving workflow.

PART I: PROFESSIONAL RECORDING IN LOGIC

Professional recording in Logic has become a natural, everyday way of life for more and more A-list bands, pop and urban producers, and classical musicians and composers. The mixing stage may still be completed in Pro Tools in some cases, but the recording is increasingly more connected to a project studio or rehearsal space where production work is being done in Logic.

Chapter 1

ADVANCED SETUP OF YOUR LOGIC STUDIO

The Basic Setup Checklist

The Logic Help files do a great job of walking you through the setup of your Logic studio. They are also covered in the first chapter of my previous book, *The Power in Logic Pro*, so the following is only a quick checklist:

- Perform a custom install using the Custom Install pane to uncheck components of the Logic content or redirect to external drives. This will conserve disk space on your internal drive.
- Connect your audio interface; download and install the current Core Audio driver from the manufacturer's website.
- Launch one of the Logic project templates from the Templates chooser when you launch the application, or afterwards from the File menu (File > New).

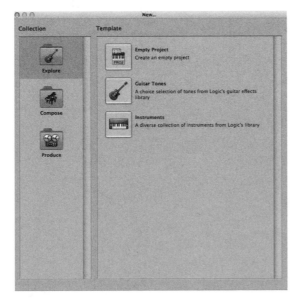

Figure 1.1: Logic project templates

- Launch Logic's audio preferences in the upper left of the toolbar to check that the audio driver was recognized (Preferences > Audio).
- To quickly check for audio playback, launch the Logic Pro Demo Project (Help > Exploring Logic Pro Demo Project). Or, on the right of the Arrange window (Media > Loops), select an Apple Loop tag and then highlight a Loop in the browser list beneath to audition it.
- Connect a MIDI controller; download and install its current driver from the manufacturer's website.
- Load a software instrument (New Track > Software Instrument). Logic will default to an electric piano preset.
- If no sound comes from your MIDI controller, check the MIDI Activity monitor in the transport that defaults to the words "No In No Out." It switches to displaying a musical note when a MIDI controller is properly connected and triggered.

Figure 1.2: MIDI Activity monitor in the transport

- If you have any issues with your MIDI or audio hardware being recognized by Logic, check the Audio MIDI Setup utility of your Mac (Applications > Utilities).
- Install any third-party instruments using the Audio Units format. If an instrument is not immediately recognized in Logic, select Reset & Rescan in Logic's Audio Units Manager.

A Deeper Look at the Recording Preferences

Logic's preferences are accessed from the toolbar in the upper left of the Arrange window. Select Audio from the pop-up menu after clicking on the Preferences button (or choosing Logic Pro > Preferences > Audio). There are two especially important tabs within the audio preferences: Devices and General. Each has a set of preferences you should at least be aware of. A few of the more notable ones are introduced below.

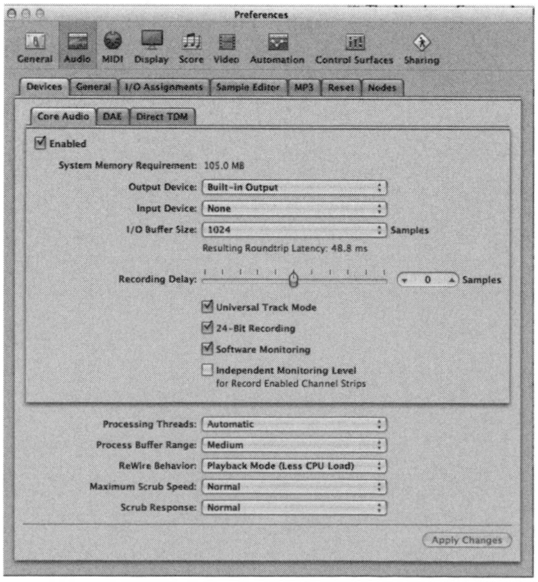

Figure 1.3: Arrange window : Preferences : Audio

Audio Preferences > Under the Devices Tab

Output Device/Input Device

Logic should automatically recognize any installed Core Audio hardware. You can confirm or otherwise select your audio interface from the pull-down menu for Audio Input Device and Output Device, and then select Apply Changes in the lower right of the dialog box.

I/O Buffer Size

The I/O buffer size is a critical audio preference. You adjust it dynamically, depending on the task. Use the lower values, such as 32 or 64 samples, while recording in order to reduce latency, and the higher values when more CPU resources are needed, such as for adding plug-ins and mixing. Understanding when and how to adjust this setting and the quality of the manufacturer's driver for your audio hardware will determine a lot about how positive your experience will be with audio in Logic.

Resulting Roundtrip Latency/Resulting Output Latency

This value is displayed directly beneath the I/O buffer size and updates depending on the current I/O buffer size. Click on the display to toggle between the two values. There is nothing for you to directly adjust; it's simply a readout.

I/O Buffer Size: 1024 ☐ Samples
Resulting Roundtrip Latency: 48.8 ms

Figure 1.4: Resulting Roundtrip Latency toggle

Universal Track Mode

This mode is a vestige of the days when professional Logic users were working with Digidesign Audio Engine (DAE) hardware. The setting is on by default and allows you to play back stereo and mono regions on a single track. Disable it only when you are using DAE hardware. To be perfectly clear, if you find yourself playing back Logic through DAE hardware, you need to disable this preference.

Software Monitoring

Keep this checkbox enabled so that you can hear the input signal, but be aware that it can introduce audible delay or latency.

Independent Monitoring Levels

This setting allows you to use the fader to adjust your monitoring level of record-enabled channel strips. When you turn off the record-enable button, the original monitoring level is restored.

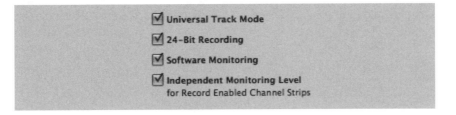

Figure 1.5: Independent monitoring level on track

Process Buffer Range

This setting is most relevant for mixing and using effects, especially with DSP cards. It is similar to the I/O buffer size in that the scale affects the amount of latency you experience. But the size and latency equation is flipped. You can choose between Small, Medium, and Large. Here, the larger the value, the more latency is introduced.

ReWire Behavior

There are different settings to choose from depending on whether you are playing back or recording with a ReWire software instrument. Playback mode uses less processing power, while Live mode uses more CPU resources, but has lower latency. Consider this preference as dynamic as the I/O buffer size if you are working with ReWire instruments. It will likely need to be adjusted each time someone programs in ReWire parts, and then reset after they have finished. The ReWire setup and workflow is covered below in this chapter.

Audio Preferences > Under the General Tab

Track Mute/Solo Behavior

This preference is an important one to be aware of and is likely a completely foreign concept to any Pro Tools user. With Fast (Remote Channel Strips) checked, clicking on a channel strip's Mute or Solo button switches the state of the associated track button, and vice versa. With CPU-saving (Slow Response) checked, the Track Mute and Solo buttons are independent of the corresponding channel strip buttons. This second option gives you the added flexibility in Logic of, if you have two tracks assigned to the same channel strip, being able to have just one of them muted or soloed. This can be incredibly helpful in the Logic workflow if, for example, you have two drum tracks from the EXS24 sampler instrument coming out of the same channel strip. You might use the same instance of the software instrument to conserve plug-in usage but keep the parts on separate tracks to allow for different velocity and quantize settings.

Plug-In Latency Compensation

Plug-in latency compensation, also referred to as plug-in delay compensation, is important when using software instruments, effects plug-ins, or DSP (digital signal processing) accelerator hardware. You can activate plug-in latency compensation for audio and software instruments or additionally for your auxes and outputs.

Logic Pro calculates the amount of latency introduced by plug-ins, and then delays audio streams by an appropriate amount—or shifts instrument and audio tracks forward in time. The recommended compensation method depends on the type of channel where the latency-inducing plug-in is being inserted. If latency-inducing plug-ins are inserted onto aux or output channels (or ReWire channels), Logic Pro delays all other audio streams by an appropriate amount. If latency-inducing plug-ins are inserted onto audio or instrument channels, Logic Pro automatically shifts these tracks forward in time. The advantage of this method is that other channels do not need to be delayed.

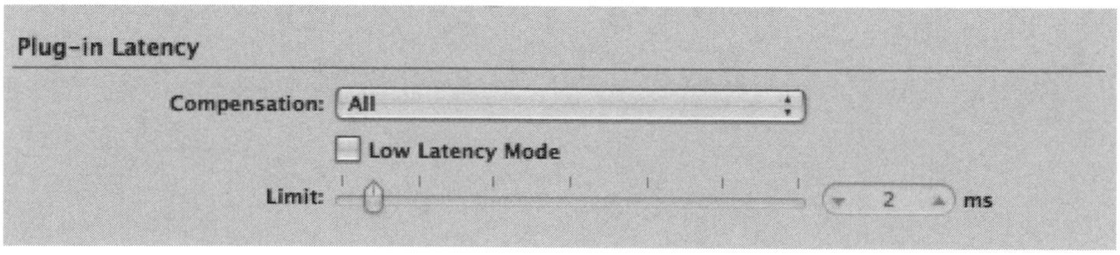

Figure 1.6: Plug-in latency compensation

Low Latency Mode Checkbox and Slider

This Low Latency Mode checkbox, directly beneath the Plug-in Latency Compensation menu, is a unique feature in Logic that can come in handy. When this preference is checked, there is a Low Latency Mode button in the transport that you can enable whenever you'd like Logic to temporarily disable any latency-inducing plug-ins, instead of having to individually bypass by Option-clicking on them when a track is record-armed.

With the Limit slider (beneath the checkbox in the audio preferences), you select how many milliseconds of latency are acceptable before plug-ins are bypassed. Bypassed plug-ins will change color from blue to orange. Note: Low Latency Mode is available for the master outputs but does not update in color!

Figure 1.7: Low Latency Mode

Thinking—and Syncing— Outside the Box

The beauty of the Logic studio is that it is so self-contained. A laptop, a pair of headphones, a flight to Maui, and you're good to go for writing a new track or remixing a record. Between the Caps Lock key trick for using the QWERTY keyboard as a music keyboard, and the killer library of software instruments and plug-ins that come with Logic, you really have a complete studio entirely inside the box.

That said, expanding your Logic studio with external hardware allows you the best of all worlds. Learning all the ways to integrate external hardware (from an Akai MPC to a stompbox to a hardware reverb) with Logic will take your workflow to the next level as a professional engineer and producer.

I was speaking recently with my longtime friend and former partner on the Apple Pro Audio team, Bill Lee, who inspired this section's subhead. Below is his ever-eloquent advice on the subject, including the steps for how to sync an Akai MPC with Logic. You'll find a few other tips from Bill throughout this book. My advice is to take every single one to heart. The chapter continues on to cover the nuts and bolts of a few other key topics with regard to integrating and synchronizing external gear.

"Thinking Outside the Box," by Bill Lee

Computers are cool. And very powerful. You can do tons of stuff "in the box," especially when it comes to making music. But there's really no substitute for some hardware gear—the gear that you love to play, tweak, tap, stomp, sweeten, mangle, and shape your music with. Here's how to incorporate your favorite hardware gear with your Logic rig to get the best of both worlds.

I/O plug-in. Let's start simple. I'm sure somewhere in your studio you have a guitar pedal or quirky old effects box that you keep around because you like the unique sound of it, and you use it occasionally on your recordings. The I/O plug-in is for you. It allows you to utilize extra connections of your audio interface to connect to your outboard hardware effects. It's the simplest plug-in in all of Logic, containing just an In setting, an Out setting, and a volume level for each. The In's and Out's correspond to the in's and out's of your audio interface. Just connect out from your audio interface into the in of your stompbox or other outboard effect, then back out of that, into the in of your audio interface. Now, your stompbox effect is a part of your plug-in chain right alongside your Logic plugs and third-party plugs. Go ahead and reorder it, bypass it, or even save the settings as a preset. I use this a lot on my master channel. I open a stereo I/O plug-in on the master channel, and go out of my audio interface into my Avalon VT-747SP EQ and Empirical Labs Fatso Jr compressor/tape simulator, then back into the audio interface. Sounds great, works great!

External instrument. Let's take it one step further. What if you have a hardware keyboard that you want to incorporate in your normal setup? The External Instrument is very similar to the I/O plug-in, but instead of going audio out and audio in, you go MIDI out (to control your keyboard), then audio in (to hear the audio outs of your keyboard). It's like having a MIDI track and an audio channel set to input all smashed into one. You can record your MIDI performance, and edit anytime you want, and you have the ability to add software plug-ins to your keyboard sound because it's now "in the box." Go ahead and dig that old FM synth out of the back of the closet, and see what I mean.

Synchronization settings. I see lots of producers and electronic musicians using drum machines like MPCs. Many of them make fantastic beats using them, then they record the beat into Logic, never ever going back to the MPC again. Furthermore, they will continue fleshing out the track, then bounce the entire thing to a stereo file, then go to another program to record vocals! Crazy! Logic is way too flexible and powerful for all of that. First, let's sync up the MPC to Logic using the synchronization settings in Logic. You will need a MIDI interface for this procedure, and to hook out from the interface into the in of your drum machine.

Here are the steps for your MPC:

Go to File > Project Settings > Synchronization > MIDI.
Select Transmit MIDI Clock—Destination 1.

In the list below you should see your MIDI interface listed. Select it. This is telling Logic to send MIDI Clock signals out of the MIDI outputs that are on your MIDI interface.

Now you need to go into your MPC (or whatever the drum machine is) and tell it to sync to MIDI clock (sometimes called MIDI beat clock, or beat clock) coming into the MIDI port that you hooked up to it.

Once the drum machine is "listening" for MIDI clock, you can hit start in Logic, and the drum machine will start playing. Even if you start from a midpoint in the song, the drum machine will chase to the same spot. Now you can work on beats in the drum machine, and keyboards, and other production in Logic all at the same time in your workflow. You can even use External Instrument to have the drum machine's audio outputs come into Logic for internal processing just as with outboard keyboards. You can sync up the onboard arpeggiator to Logic's tempo using this method. And then, don't forget to go ahead and record the vocals at anytime you're ready. No need to bounce the beat, or the track, or anything. Everything works fine together. Just create!

With these few simple features, you can combine your software and hardware gear easily to have a simplified nonstop workflow. Keep it moving! —*Bill Lee, (producer-engineer, Dubspot NYC instructor, former Apple Logic Pro clinician)*

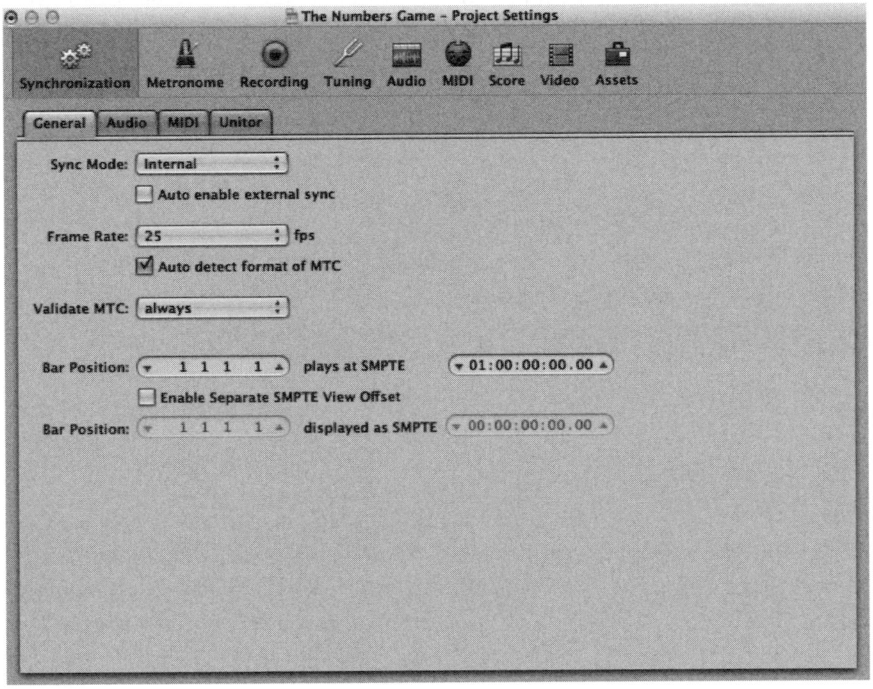

Figure 1.8: Project Settings: Synchronization

Synchronizing an MPC and Other External Clocks

The Synchronization settings are relevant when using Logic with another computer or any other external hardware that has a transport and clock. Synchronization settings are specific to a project. You can access them from the File menu in the Arrange window (File > Project Settings > Synchronization), or you can click on the Settings button in the Arrange toolbar and then Synchronization in the pop-up menu.

Under the General Settings tab, set the Sync Mode to Internal if Logic is the master clock, or to External if Logic is running as a slave, which is rarely advised. If you do plan to slave Logic to an MPC—again not advised—be sure to enable the checkbox next to the Auto Enable External Sync setting.

More Sync Settings to Know About

The Synchronization settings are relevant when using Logic with another computer or other external hardware that has a transport and clock. One scenario I've confronted (though I don't recommend) is producers syncing two laptops during the writing process so both can work independently on parts, and then immediately integrate them. More common, of course, is the integration of a drum machine, like the MPC. To set Synchronization for a specific project, click on the Settings button in the Arrange toolbar, and then on Synchronization in the pop-up menu (or choose File > Project Settings > Synchronization).

In the General Preferences tab, set the Sync Mode to Internal so that Logic is the master clock, or to External if Logic is running as a slave (which is rarely advised). If you do plan to slave Logic to an MPC—again not advised—be sure to enable the checkbox next to the Auto Enable External Sync setting.

External Synchronization

Logic is by default set to Internal Sync—master mode. The Transport bar's Sync button can be used to synchronize Logic to a sync source. When enabled, the transport button and bar ruler both glow blue.

Figure 1.9: Transport bar's Sync button

The Fine Print of Quarter Frame Accuracy

All of the SMPTE settings are well detailed in the Help files. There is one caveat regarding sync in Logic. When slaving Logic to another DAW, the device will not be sample accurate since Logic only supports MTC for sync, which is inherently quarter-frame accurate. The accuracy varies but can in fact be better than quarter frame. The variance is caused by the jitter in the MIDI stream coming down the USB pipe of the MIDI interface.

The only time this whole sample-accuracy business becomes an issue is when or if you are transferring tracks from another multitrack medium like Pro Tools to Logic, and you have to do it in multiple passes. For example, say that you have a 48-track Pro Tools session that you're passing over to Logic via a 32-input audio interface. You transfer 32 tracks first, and then come back and do the remaining 16. That second set of 16 tracks will be off by up to a few hundred samples. Even that is not a huge issue—200 samples would be ~4.5 ms. It's primarily a problem if any of the tracks in the first set of transferred tracks were recorded live with tracks in the second set of transfer tracks. In that case, you might get some phase issues. For example, if you were tracking live a full kit of multitracked drums—you'd strategically want to keep those tracks in the same transfer pass when at all possible.

ReWire in Logic (is easy)

ReWire is the communication protocol developed by Propellerhead (www.propellerheads.se) for synchronizing audio and MIDI data between applications.

ReWire setup is easier than ever, and the workflow integration is extremely fluid inside Logic. That said, you either love it, live with it, or avoid it. It's a necessity and convenience in the modern world of DAWs, where a producer's workflow involves combining the palette from more than one DAW.

Any ReWire-compatible application is either a host or a client at any given time—you can't ReWire a client into a host and simultaneously ReWire that into another host. Although there can be only one host, you can usually ReWire multiple clients into that host.

Here are a few basics of ReWire:

- The client's audio outputs stream into the host's mixer.
- The host and client transports are linked so that starting or stopping either one starts or stops the other, respectively.
- Setting loop points in either application affects both applications.
- Both applications can share the same audio interface.

ReWire programs must be opened in a particular order. First launch the host, which will be Logic, and then launch any clients. Close programs in the reverse order. You won't break anything if you don't follow this protocol, but if you open the client first, Logic will fail to see it. If you try to close the host first, you won't be allowed to because it will still have an open connection with the client. By opening the host (Logic) and then the slave (Reason or Live), a sync connection is established. Transport controls in either application will cause the other to start, stop, and play along in sync.

Accessing a ReWire Instrument

There are two parts to the setup of a ReWire instrument in Logic: the MIDI control and the audio routing—both of which are practically instantaneous.

First, create an External MIDI track in the New Tracks dialog box.

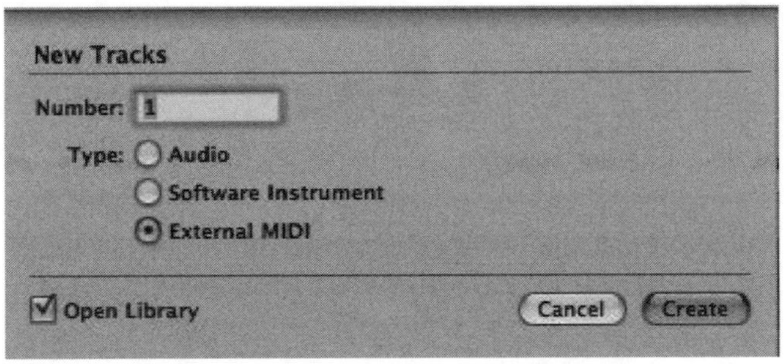

Figure 1.10: External instrument track for a ReWire instrument

Under the Library tab to the right of the Arrange window, you will immediately see the ReWire application (such as Reason or Live). Double-click on the application to open it. Then, all the available ReWire instruments from the respective app will be visible in the Library. Click on the instrument you want in order to select it, and you are ready to play.

Next up is the audio routing into Logic, which is effortless. ReWire instruments that are introduced as an external instrument will show up automatically as inputs to auxiliary channels.

Power Tip: Preference to Reduce Latency with ReWire

Before you start programming with the ReWire instrument, you may want to launch the Audio Preferences to adjust the latency setting in the ReWire Behavior tab, explained earlier in this chapter under Audio Preferences > Devices.

Aggregate Device Seatup for Multiple Audio Interfaces

This is an awesome lifesaver when you find yourself in a situation where you need more inputs or outputs than a single audio interface can offer. You can combine any two or more interfaces that have Core Audio drivers.

This versatile Core Audio feature is not available for DAE hardware, so it is often unfamiliar to Pro Tools engineers. In the Audio MIDI Setup Utility, you can create an Aggregate Device Setup to use more than one audio interface at a time in Logic, GarageBand, or other Core Audio–compliant applications. Here are the steps:

- Launch the Audio MIDI Setup utility.
- From the Audio menu, choose Open Aggregate Device Editor.
- Click on the "+" (plus sign) under the Aggregate Devices list to create a new empty device.
- Highlight the device name to rename it.
- All connected interfaces appear in the Structure area below.
- Select the ones you want in the Aggregate Setup by checking the Use checkbox.
- You can reorder them here as well to determine the sequence of inputs and outputs, which are visible in the Input and Output columns.
- The built-in input and output can be selected as an audio interface in an aggregate setup.
- Select which device you want to provide the master clock in the furthest column to the left with the radio button.
- In Logic's audio preferences, select the Aggregate Device under the Input and Output Device. You will see it listed using whatever name you gave it in the Audio MIDI Setup utility.

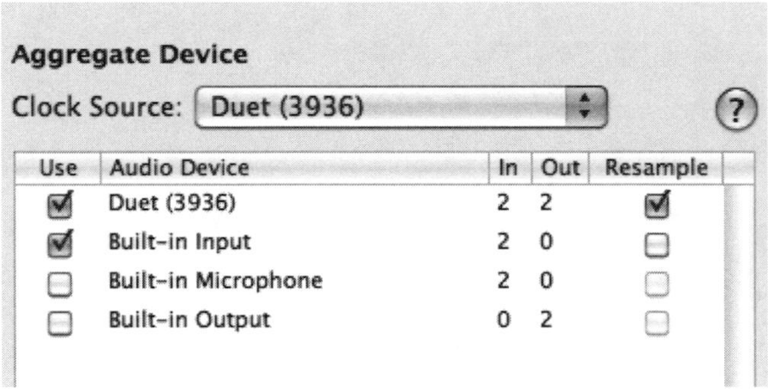

Figure 1.11: Aggregate Device setup

Power Tip: Aggregate Device Outputs with Multiple Interfaces

The outputs in the Aggregate Device Editor will be numbered from the top down in Logic. You can drag them up or down to change the order and numbering.

Power Tip: Uniform Sample Rate with Aggregate Devices

All devices must be set to the same sampling rate, or else the aggregate setup won't work!

Chapter 2
ADVANCED AUDIO RECORDING

The task at hand is to get you driving as a recording engineer in Logic, and fast—whether you've used the application before or not. This is completely doable if you focus, read, and, as soon as possible, try out what you read.

A Superfast Tour of the Logic Workspace

After you read this section, "A Superfast Tour of the Logic Workspace," consider yourself as having been issued a learner's permit to drive in Logic. The section "Basic Audio Recording" will be your license to record. But no skimming or speeding when you read!

The Arrange Window: Your Workspace

Logic has a one-window workspace called the Arrange window where the project arrangement is built. All the editors (Mixer, Score, Piano Roll, and so on) and Media area are accessed from here. A lot of Logic users don't even know that the main workspace is called the Arrange window, but it is.

Figure 2.1: The Arrange window

Your Project Template to Get Started

From the File > New menu, select an Empty Project template or a template you created yourself in the Template window that is ready to roll for recording or mixing with your external hardware integrated, or preloaded with any favorite software instruments or effects plug-ins you like to have available in every session (for example, drum kit, acoustic piano, funky bass, vocal plug-in chain for your singer, your guitar, and so on).

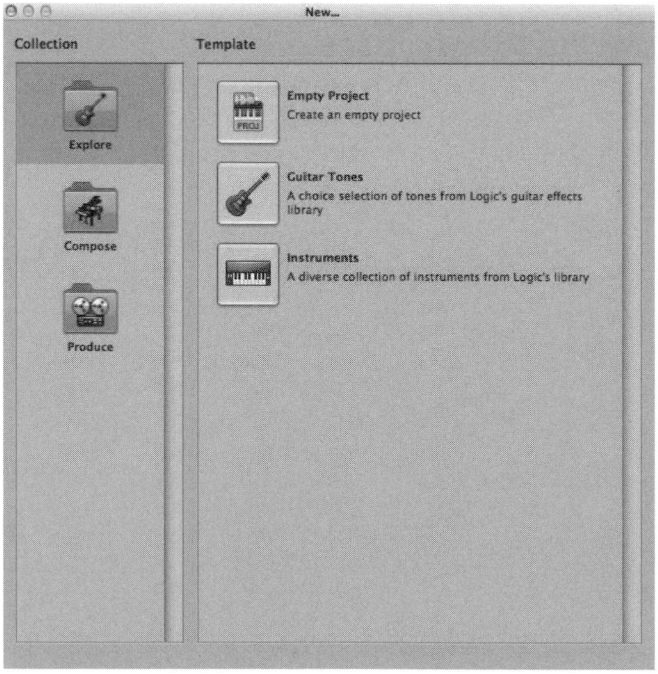

Figure 2.2: The Empty Project template

Track List, Track Header, and New Tracks Button

The track list contains a list of your audio tracks and software instrument tracks. Control-click on any track name in the list to configure the track header. This will allow you to choose which objects are visible in the track list.

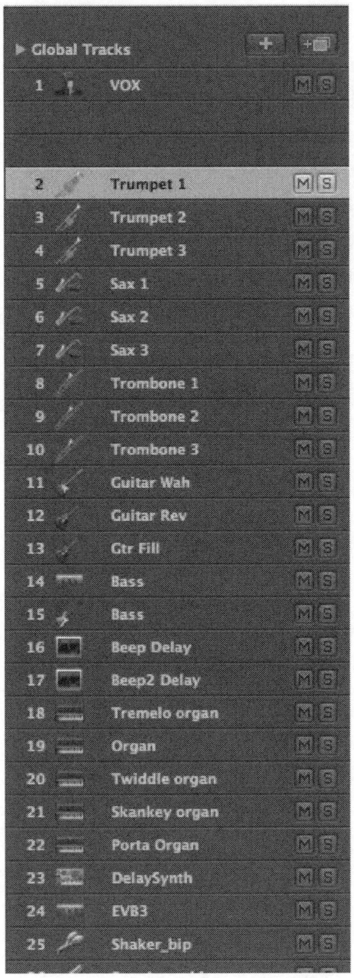

Figure 2.3: The track list and track header

Use the Create Track button—the "+" sign above the track list—to add more tracks, whether for audio or for software instruments. The button on the right, labeled New Track With Duplicate Settings, adds new tracks with all the same plug-ins loaded and pan/volume settings as the currently highlighted track.

Figure 2.4: Create Track button

The Transport and Basic Playback Controls

The Transport bar is at the bottom of the Arrange window. Customize it by Control-clicking in any empty gray or directly on any buttons or controls in the Transport bar to access the sheet of buttons you can add to the Transport bar area. Besides hitting Play with the transport button, you can enable playback by clicking the playhead in the lower half of the bar ruler.

Clicking anywhere in the Arrange workspace with the Marquee tool creates a thin white insertion point that enables song playback at that exact location, overriding a cycle area. This is especially convenient to Pro Tools users who not used to moving the mouse all the way up to the bar ruler to engage playback. (See the section "The Essential Marquee Tool," in chapter 3, "Navigating and Editing: The Marquee Tool and Beyond.") A final way to navigate to a specific location in the timeline and ready your project for recording or playback is to use the key command Go To (Position), which I reassign to the G key because I use it so often and that's logical to me. See the section "Key Commands: The Secret to Learning Logic (condensed)," in chapter 10.

The Media

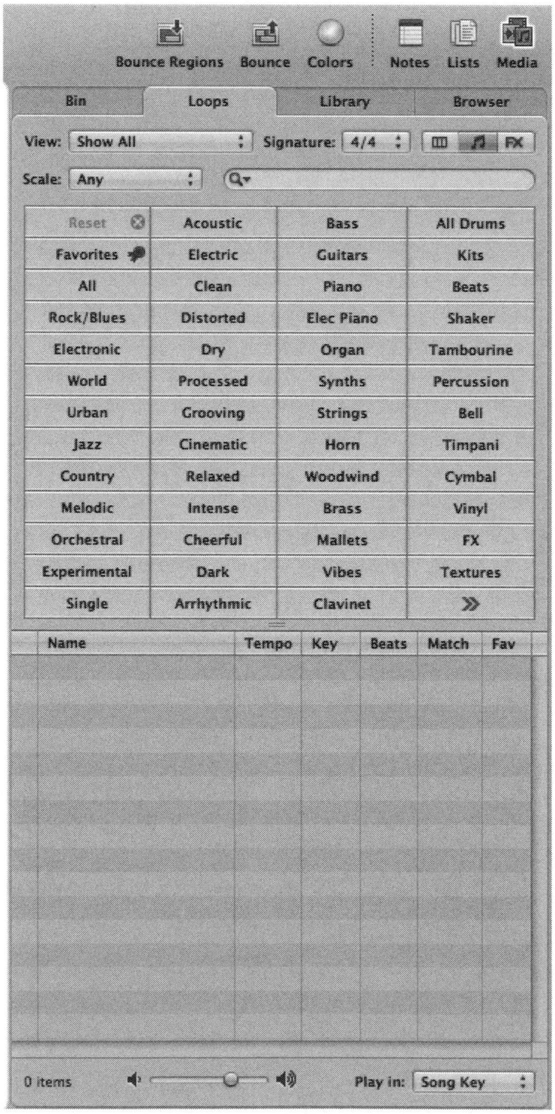

Figure 2.5: The Media area

The area to the right in the Arrange window is your entry point to all content for your project, whether inside your Logic project folder or somewhere else on your hard drive. The tabs on top of the Media area are labeled Bin, Loops, Library, and Browser. These contain, respectively, all the audio files associated with your project, Apple Loops, the library of channel strip settings (which contain factory plug-in chains and ones you design yourself), and a portal to your drive and connected drives from the browser. This is also where track import is handled. Note the Add button in the lower right corner that looks like a "+" (plus symbol) for the track import features.

The Bar Ruler, Toolbar, and Tool Menus

The bar ruler on top of the Arrange window is your timeline displaying bars, beats, or SMPTE as well as your cycle area. The toolbar above the bar ruler has a number of icons that are shortcuts to various tasks in Logic, many of which are also available as key commands. Control-click to customize.

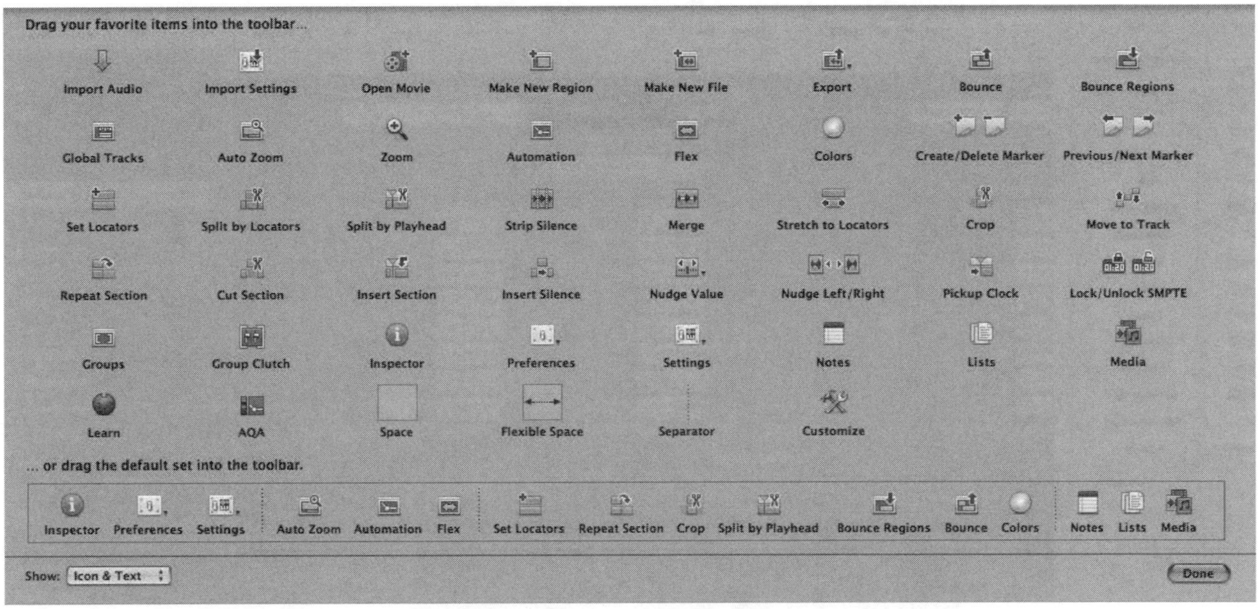

Figure 2.6: Customizing the toolbar

The Tool menus at the upper right corner of the Arrange window are where you assign your primary tool (the tool on left) and your secondary or Command-click tool (the tool on right).

Figure 2.7: The Tool menus

Otherwise, your primary tool can be selected and switched from the floating toolbox accessed with the Escape key. The floating toolbox will appear wherever your Pointer tool is on the screen, and so it can be a very fast way to switch tools.

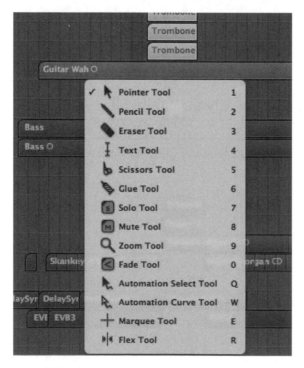

Figure 2.8: The floating toolbox via the Escape key

The Mixer and Other Main Editors

Click on the editor tabs at the bottom of the Arrange window to access the Mixer, Sample Editor, and the three MIDI editors: the Piano Roll, Score, and Hyper Editor.

Figure 2.9: The Mixer, Sample Editor, and three MIDI editors

The Dual Channel Strips' Awesomeness

The two channel strips in the Arrange window to the left are brilliant. The channel strip to the left is the mixer channel for the highlighted track in the Arrange window. When a bus is inserted on one of its sends, the channel strip to the right updates to display the next available aux track. This channel strip to the right otherwise represents your main outs by default. To restore the default view of the channel strip to the right, click on the Stereo Out pane on the selected track's channel strip on the left. Clever right?

That's it!

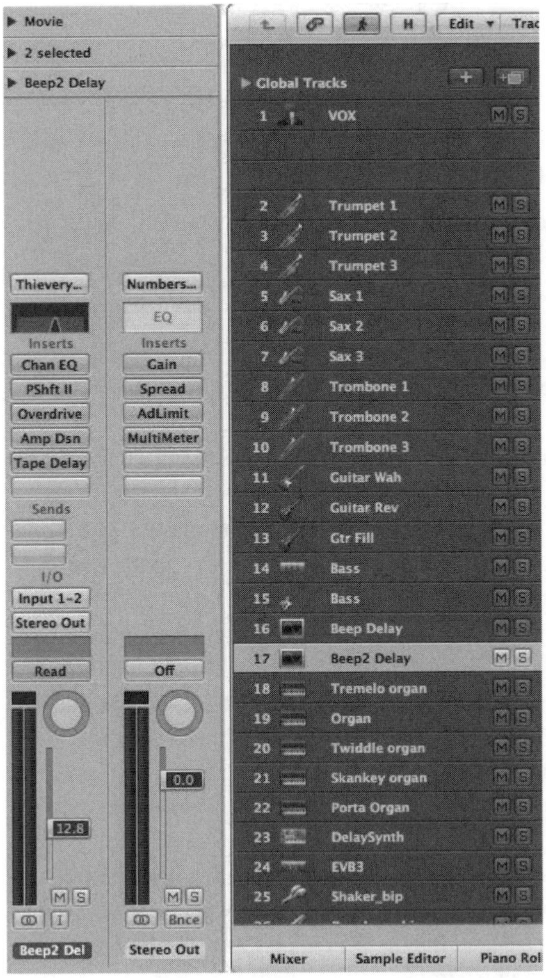

Figure 2.10: Dual channel strips in the Arrange window

Power Tip: Waveform Zoom Button

If I had a nickel for how many times I've had to show this, I'd definitely be rich. Directly beneath the Arrange workspace, to the right of the left/right scrollbar, is the Waveform Zoom button, which you use to adjust the scale of the waveform on a track. The icon for this function is a waveform. Click on the icon, and a transparent vertical slider pops up. Drag up on the slider, and the waveform increases in size making it easier to view the peaks for editing; drag down, and the waveform decreases in scale.

This same Waveform Zoom button can be used to visually resize the waveform in the Beat Mapping track, which is introduced in the section "Beat Mapping to Create a Tempo Map," in chapter 6.

Figure 2.11: Adjusting waveform size in the Arrange window

Basic Audio Recording in Logic

Here's a quick checklist for preparing to record, from setting the click and count-in to naming tracks. For more detail, check either the Logic Help files or chapter 4 of *The Power in Logic Pro*.

Record Setup Checklist

- Create new audio tracks in the Arrange window with the New Track button (which looks like a "+" sign) at the top of the track list.
- Select the Record Enable button (labeled with an "R") on a channel strip or on the record track in the track list so that track(s) are armed.
- Check levels on the fader and make necessary adjustments from the input of your signal chain (hardware mixer, mic pre, converter, and so on). You should also see the meter jumping in the track list, to the left of the track name in the track header.
- Set the record path to your Logic "project" (how Logic songs are referred to) in the Save As dialog box (File > Save As).
- Click-and-hold on the Record button in the transport to open Recording Settings and adjust count-in, or launch Recording Settings and then select Metronome Settings. Set 8th- or 16th-note clicks here by enabling Division in Metronome Settings.
- In Audio Settings, assign the sample rate for recording (Arrange toolbar > Settings > Audio).
- Name tracks in the track list before recording so that files are properly named in the Audio Bin. See the Power Tip below by Bill Lee, "Tab Key to Name Next Track/Channel," on track naming, and the "Managing the Audio Bin" section in chapter 10 if you forget to properly name or otherwise need to rename a track.

- Set your playhead to where you'd like recording to begin, if not at the top of the project. See tips above for navigating in the Transport bar.

Record

- Select the Record button in the Transport bar, or press the default command, the R key.

Overdubs

- **Punching-in:** In playback mode, use the default key command Shift + R to toggle record. Press it again to drop out of record and resume playback. Special Note: The Punch on the Fly setting must also be enabled by clicking-and-holding the Record button in the Transport bar, and selecting this option from the pop-up menu.
- **Autopunch:** In the transport, enable the Autopunch button, which has two small arrows—one pointing upward and one downward. A shaded red area will appear in the bar ruler beneath the cycle area defined by left and right locators. Drag to adjust its length.
- **Replace Record:** Turn on the Replace button in the Transport bar and record-arm the track with the Record Enable button on the track you want to record. The Replace button has an icon of an "X" in the center. A new recording replaces the original recording (or a portion of it) and is stored as a new region. The original region data between the punch-in and punch-out points is deleted. Cycle recording in Replace mode only deletes regions from the first cycle pass from punch-in to punch-out point or end of the cycle.

Figure 2.12: Replace button in Transport bar

Power Tip: Tab Key to Name Next Track/Channel

Prepping a new project for recording? Here's a quick way to get through your track naming. Double-click on a track header, name it, then hit Tab. That will go to the next track and highlight the name so you can rename it. Type, Tab, Type, Tab, etc. Nice and quick. —*Bill Lee*

Monitoring in Logic

The monitoring features in Logic effectively take into account all recording situations to ensure efficient and flexible delay compensation.

Low Latency Mode

Low Latency mode allows you to limit the acceptable delay time caused by plug-ins while recording by temporarily bypassing plug-ins that exceed the limit you designate. This is a great feature for recording a quick overdub after you've already started the mixing stage or have otherwise been layering plug-ins. Plug-ins are bypassed to ensure a maximum delay across the signal flow if a track remains under the chosen value. There is no comparable feature in Pro Tools, though there is delay compensation, and on TDM/HD there is pretty much zero delay so this would not be an issue.

Low Latency Mode Setup:

- Enable the Low Latency Mode checkbox in Audio Preferences > General.
- Adjust the Limit slider beneath the checkbox to the desired level of milliseconds of latency across the track's signal path.
- Toggle the Low Latency button in the transport as needed when an audio track is record-armed if any latency is experienced. The Low Latency button is located directly to the left of the Cycle button, on the right side of the Transport area.

Figure 2.13: Low Latency mode

Auto Input Monitoring

This allows you to hear the input signal only during recording. Before and afterward you'll hear the previously recorded audio on the track. If it's disabled, you will always hear the input signal.

To enable, select Options > Audio > Auto Input Monitoring from the menu bar, or control-click on the Record button in the Transport bar and choose Auto Input Monitoring from the pop-up menu.

Input Monitoring

The Input Monitoring button on the track allows you to monitor any tracks that are not record-armed. Enable the Input Monitoring button on the track header of an audio track or on the channel strip in the Arrange window or Mixer. This button can be left enabled during or after recording. Keep in mind that Input Monitoring will introduce some latency, depending on your audio hardware and driver settings.

Figure 2.14: The Input Monitoring button on the track header

Power Tip: Combining Input Monitoring with Auto Input Monitoring

If Input Monitoring is enabled, you will always hear incoming audio, even if Auto Input Monitoring is turned on.

Monitoring Level/Independent Monitoring Level

If Independent Monitoring for Record Enabled Channel Strips is enabled in the Audio Preferences, you can adjust the monitor level from the fader. When the record button is disabled, the original playback level is restored. As always with a DAW, the volume fader controls the playback (monitoring level, not the record level). Input levels must be adjusted at the source on your audio interface, mic pres, and so on.

Software Monitoring

This allows you to monitor plug-ins inserted onto an armed audio channel strip. An audio input must be assigned for software monitoring to be available. Effects plug-ins are only monitored, not recorded. To monitor a track with effects plug-ins, be sure that

Software Monitoring is enabled in the Audio Preferences > Devices tab. In Pro Tools, you can always hear HD/TDM plug-ins on a track that's set to Input, while the RTAS plug-ins disengage when you are in Input mode.

Takes Recordings and the Take Folder

Multitake recording to a take folder is automatically achieved by recording again on the same track. As soon as a second recording takes place over the first audio region, a take folder is created on a single audio track in the Arrange window. The take folder is created automatically when you record over existing audio as long as Replace mode is not enabled. This allows you to choose afterward which parts of the different performances you want to keep. Takes recording is available for both audio and MIDI tracks.

To record multiple takes without stopping, turn on Cycle mode with the button in the Transport bar or the default key command, C, and define the cycle area. Once you stop recording, you can always record again over a take folder, which will record new takes and not erase the old takes. The only situation in which new takes are not recorded is when Replace Record, which has the symbol of an "X," is enabled in the transport.

A sideways-pointing triangle in the upper left of the region header indicates the take folder; click on the downward-pointing triangle in upper right to reveal the takes. Editing inside the take folder is covered in chapter 4, "Quick Swipe Comping."

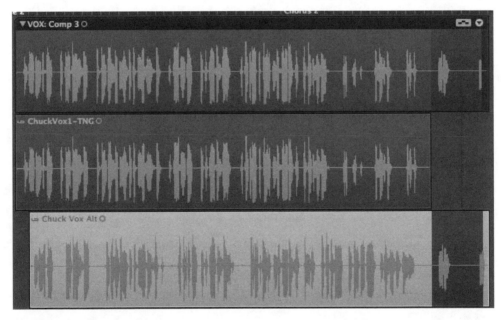

Figure 2.15: The take folder

Multitrack Recording Scenarios: Groups and Folders

Whether you are multitrack recording in the studio or in a mobile recording situation, Logic has made it very easy to create the tracks you need to get started. When creating a new recording project, there is the automatic dialog box to sort how many audio tracks and software instrument tracks. Then, that same dialog box is easily accessed with the Add Track button at the top of the track list to adjust inputs and outputs. To record to multiple audio tracks simultaneously, record-enable all the intended tracks in the track list. Set each one to a different input. Take folders can be created on each of these audio tracks at the same time if you record over the same regions.

Figure 2.16: Recording to multiple tracks

Logic has some very advanced features for recording large sessions. Track grouping is handled a bit differently in Logic than in Pro Tools, but the fundamental workflow that is explained next should sound familiar. Keep an open mind to this alternative of using folders. I've spoken with more than a few engineers who swear by Logic's folder system.

Working with Track Groups

Track groups are useful for every stage of engineering—recording, editing, and mixing—so it is best to introduce early on.

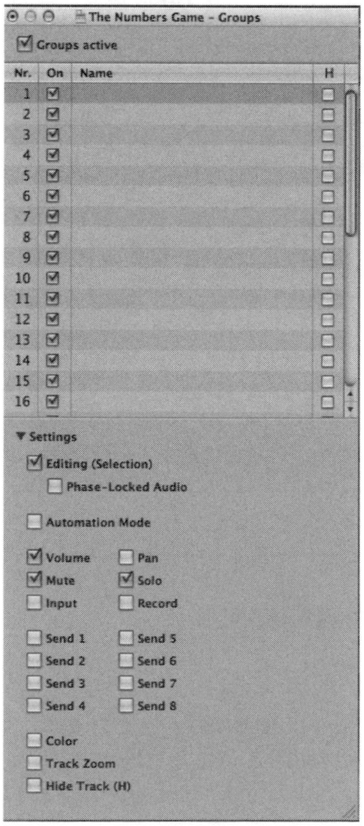

Figure 2.17: Assignable settings for a group

Creating a Group

To create a track group in Logic, click-and-hold in the gray-shaded pane on a track's channel strip just above the fader and panner, and the Group pull-down menu will be revealed. There you can create a new group, name it, and select which parameters will be active.

To assign a channel strip to multiple groups, press Shift while creating a group in the Group menu. The group slot displays the combination of group numbers that the channel strip is assigned to. The grouping pane on each channel strip reveals the group assignment at a glance.

Figure 2.18:
Assigning
channel strip to
multiple groups

Disabling Groups: Group Clutch

To temporarily disable all groups, choose Options > Group Clutch or use the Toggle Group Clutch key command. The default assignment is Command + G. When Group Clutch is enabled, all group slots change color—from yellow (active) to light gray (temporarily disabled).

Figure 2.19:
Disabling groups
with Group
Clutch

Group Settings

The group settings are self-explanatory as far as Volume, Mute, Solo, Pan, Color, Track Zoom, and so on. One noteworthy setting is the Editing submenu with the Phase-Locked Audio checkbox. Everything within the group will stay in phase while editing.

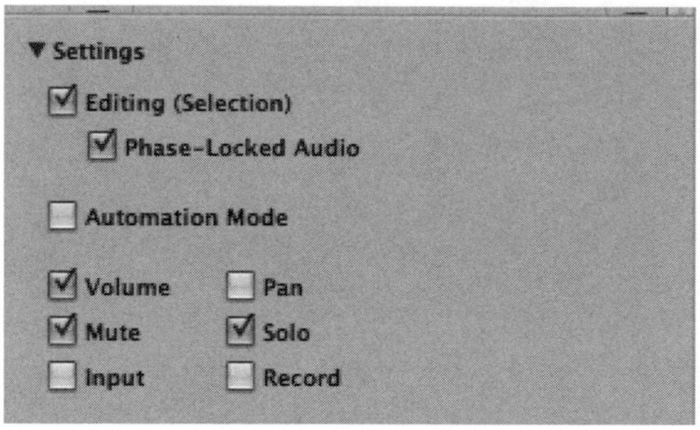

Figure 2.20: Group Settings window

An Alternative: Aux Track Groups

Another way to create subgroups is to use sends and aux channel strips. The advantage here is that you have a channel strip in the mixer that all tracks in the group are routed to for adjusting volume, pan, mute, and adding effects.

Folders: For Boys with Big Logic Projects

> I use folders in Logic to clean up tracks when I'm cutting vocals. When I have 30 vocal tracks of other takes and versions, or come back and want to recut a vocal, I'll take the old vocals and put them in a folder and name that. And I usually color it, too.
> —Rick Sheppard (Dallas Austin's engineer for Janet Jackson, Gwen Stefani, TLC, Madonna and many more)

The folder is an organizational tool that is unique to Logic for group recording, editing, and mixing. Many Pro Tools users have eyed this track management technique with envy. Folders are particularly helpful when you are working with large projects that have dozens of vocals and drum tracks. Just as the name suggests, you can pack a group of tracks into a folder that might be labeled Vocals, Drums, and so on, which will take up the same space as a single track in the Arrange window but will contain multiple tracks that can be edited simultaneously.

A folder is technically a region that contains other regions, just like any other folder on a Mac viewed from the Finder. A closed folder looks like a MIDI region, with horizontal lines representing the data contained within.

Figure 2.21: A collapsed folder view from the Arrange area

When the folder is opened, the workspace looks just like the Arrange area and track list of any Logic project, except that you are seeing only the track contents of the folder. You can also use folders to represent entire songs for putting together a concert, or sections of a song (for example, verse or chorus) to experiment with the song arrangement.

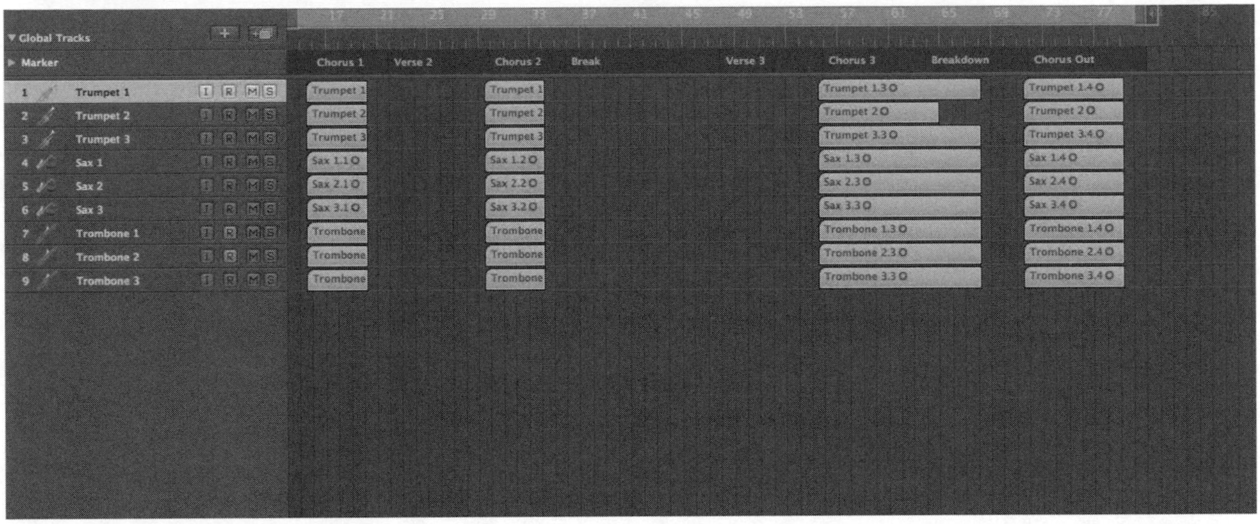

Figure 2.22: The view inside a Logic folder

Packing and unpacking folders

- To pack a folder, select the desired regions for the folder.
- In the local Region menu, choose Folder, and then Pack Folder or press the default key command Shift + Command + F (or choose Arrange > Regions > Folder > Pack Folder).
- To unpack a folder, choose Region > Folder > Unpack Folder. All tracks of the project are displayed in the Arrange window again.

When you are working inside a folder, the folder track itself is not visible. The Arrange title bar shows the project name and the folder title. To jump inside the folder, double-click in the folder region. To return to the Arrange window from inside the folder, double-click in the empty space outside of any track. The folder will collapse, and the Arrange window will be back in view.

PART II: THE ANATOMY OF EDITING IN LOGIC

Let's be honest. Editing audio in Logic often gets a bad rap, but the truth is that many aspects of it are quite detailed and effective for working quickly if you take the time to learn and practice the key commands and editing tools relevant to your workflow. Read the next four chapters, and you'll be on your way to incredible efficiency and speed when editing in Logic.

Chapter 3

NAVIGATING AND EDITING

Becoming Master of the Logic Transport

Pro Tools has only two main transport controls: play and play from previous play position. Something as basic as navigating the Logic transport often throws a Pro Tools user off. Our resident Logic friend Bill Lee eloquently explains below how Pro Tools users can avoid that pitfall in their quest to orient themselves in Logic by using the Transport Button menu to customize the transport. Control-click in the Transport Bar area to access the Customize Transport Bar menu.

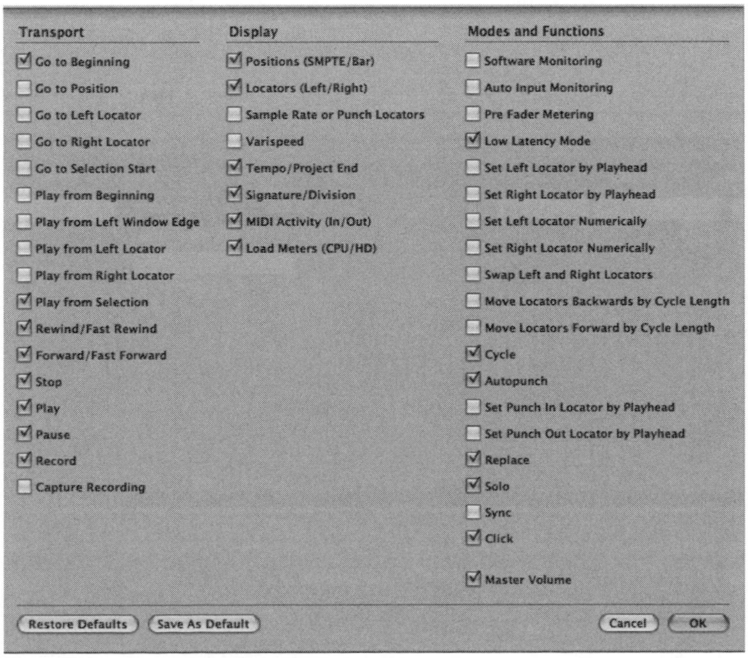

Figure 3.1: Customizing the Transport bar

This tip is for everyone, but especially for folks who are coming to Logic from Pro Tools or another DAW. The default Pro Tools playback behavior is to play only what is currently selected in the edit page. The Logic default behavior is to play wherever the playhead is regardless of region selection. If you would like to change this behavior to your exact preference, click-and-hold on the Play button in the Transport bar. There you will see a menu that gives you options for exactly what happens when you hit play. There is another menu under the Stop button, as well as the Cycle button. Under the Cycle button, notice the Auto Select Locators option. This will act like Pro Tools, and whatever region you have selected is the area of the song that will play. Check 'em all out. —*Bill Lee*

The Pointer Tool and the Tool Menus

This chapter assumes that you are familiar with the Pointer tool (the primary tool in Logic that has an icon shaped like an arrow) and the Tool menus (located in the upper right of the Arrange window for selecting your main tool and for assigning your Command-click tool).

You can always temporarily grab any tool from the primary menu on the left of the Tool menus. However, a key to working fast in Logic is to make an assignment in the secondary Tool menu located on the right. To access the alternate tool, hold down the Command key, which is why it is formally referred to as the Command-click tool.

The Marquee tool is your most important tool in Logic outside of the Pointer tool. Be sure to read this next section carefully, and really practice the navigation and editing shortcuts that the Marquee tool offers.

The Essential Marquee Tool

The Marquee tool is perhaps the most powerful editing tool in Logic, and it also provides some cool behaviors for navigation. The symbol for the Marquee tool is a "+" (plus sign).

Figure 3.2: The Marquee tool

For Pro Tools users, the Marquee tool is most closely related to the Selector tool. Therefore, with the Pointer tool as the main tool in Logic and the Marquee tool as the alternate tool, you are most closely replicating the Pro Tools Smart Tool (Hand, Trim, and Selector Tools).

Using the Marquee tool, drag across a region or multiple regions across tracks to select. Then, you can quickly perform various edit functions such as creating dropouts by muting or deleting parts of a region. You can always extend the start and end point of your Marquee selection with the Shift key. What's fantastic is how easy it is to apply Marquee tool edits in real time while the transport is running and you're listening back to your project. Especially if there are other musicians in the room, you don't need to interrupt the groove by stopping the music to perform an edit.

Spend some time experimenting with the following powerful Marquee tool navigation and edit functions:

- **Marquee Cut:** Marquee-select across an area of a region or of multiple regions, and then click into the Marquee-selected area with the Pointer tool by releasing the Command key (if Marquee is your alternate tool). The area will be snipped on either side, creating an independent region. Or, double-click with your Marquee to make an incision into a region. This will cut the region into two regions.

- With Marquee Cut, there is rarely any reason to use the older Scissors tool for basic cutting. The Scissors tool requires two separate incisions on either side of an area in order to isolate it into a new region.

- **Marquee Mute:** Marquee-select across an area of a region or of multiple regions, and then press the M key to mute the selection. Both sides of the highlighted area will be cut creating an independent region—or independent regions if you are swiping across tracks.

- **Marquee + Option + Copy:** Marquee-select across an area of a region or of multiple regions, and then Option-drag to copy the highlighted area to another place in the timeline on the same track or onto another track. The cut from the Marquee selection will be automatically "healed" and will no longer be visible.

- **Marquee-Selection Paste:** The Marquee selection can be an insertion point for pasting content from the clipboard. When you click-and-hold with the Marquee tool, a help tag appears indicating what the bars/beats of your location are so that you can make an exact selection in time to place the region or note events.

- **Single Pixel Marquee:** If you don't know this one, read this section carefully! Click into the Arrange workspace with the Marquee tool to create a thin white vertical line. When you press the Spacebar to enable playback, the playhead will jump to the single-pixel marquee insertion point. Even if there is a cycle area selected in the bar ruler, the single-pixel point will take priority as to where playback will start. To remove the single-pixel mark, click anywhere in the workspace with the Pointer tool.

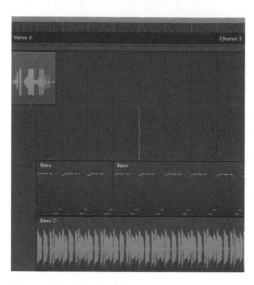

Figure 3.3: Single-pixel marquee

- **Single Pixel Marquee and Delete key to cut:** Click into a region in the Arrange workspace with the Marquee tool to create a thin white vertical line. Then, select the Delete key on your keyboard. A cut will be made in the region.
- **Marquee Swipe and Marquee Stripe:** Swipe across multiple tracks with the Marquee tool to create a region selection across all the tracks. Then click into the highlighted area with the Pointer tool by releasing the Command key—if Marquee is your alternate tool. Or, after making a Marquee tool selection, select Mute with the key command M. This is a great trick for creating a breakdown for one beat, two beats, or a whole bar. Or, activate the Marquee Stripe area in the bar ruler by clicking on the music note in the upper right of the Arrange window, just below the Tool menus. Once Marquee Stripe is enabled here, you can drag across the upper area of the bar ruler to define a Marquee selection across tracks.

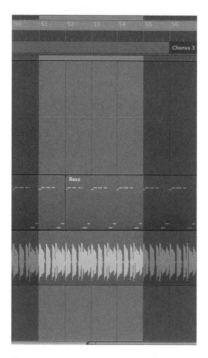

Figure 3.4: Marquee Stripe in bar ruler

- **Marquee-Select Empty Space:** This is a big one. When you cut, copy, or paste a Marquee selection, the empty space in the selection is included. This is perfect for editing regions that don't start on the downbeat of a bar or even right on a beat. After making the selection, you must apply the keystrokes Command + C to copy, and then Command + V to paste at the new location. Unfortunately, Option-drag does not work in this situation for copying the selected area.

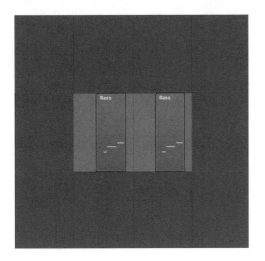

Figure 3.5: Marquee-select empty space

- **Set Locators by Marquee:** Set a cycle area by your Marquee selection simply by clicking on the Set Locators tool in the toolbar after making a Marquee selection. This Set Locators tool works for regions as well. Once selected, you can easily repeat, insert, and cut within the locators.
- **Marquee Snap to Transients (Tab to Transient):** "Tab to Transient" is the Pro Tools term for using the Tab key to jump forward and backward between transients. Transients are the peaks in your audio when you are completely zoomed in. Logic implemented a similar feature with the Marquee tool.

Figure 3.6: Set locators by Marquee selection

Click into the audio file with the Marquee tool, then use your Left and Right Arrow keys to jump to the previous and next transient respectively. It's helpful to be zoomed in enough to really view the transients.

If there is a Marquee tool selection, the Right and Left Arrows adjust the end of the selection, snapping to transients. Shift + Left Arrow/Right Arrow behaves similarly for the left selection border.

- **Marquee Cut on Transient:** A quick editing technique is to press the Delete key after selecting a transient to make a cut on that transient. Another power trick is to Shift-select between two transients with the Marquee tool so that the area between is shaded. Then, use the Delete key to quickly slice on both sides and create a region.

- **Quick Swipe Marquee Record:** If you have audio on a track and want to record over a section, Marquee-select the part you want to punch in, and then press Record. The Autopunch light will come on in the transport. It drops into Record mode but records only over the part selected with the Marquee tool. This achieves the same results as enabling Autopunch in the transport, then adjusting the thin cycle area in the bar ruler.

- **Marquee-Select Automation:** Automation has not been covered yet, but this is a great Marquee tool trick. Marquee-select any area of automation, then when you click back in with the Pointer tool, four nodes are created to easily draw in volume rides. See the section "Writing and Editing Track Automation Data" in chapter 8 for more details on automation in Logic.

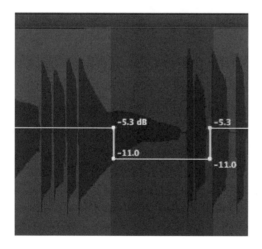

Figure 3.7: Marquee-select automation

Power Trick from Bill Lee:
Forward/Rewind/Cut by Transient with Marquee

Now that you're familiar with the Marquee tool, be sure you know that you can click in your audio region with the Marquee tool and just cursor left or right to move the marquee insertion to the next or previous transient. And you can cut at the point of the marquee insertion with the Delete key. Try it. Once you start using it, you'll be hooked. —*Bill Lee*

Navigating at Full Speed

Navigating in Logic is astonishingly fast when you take a minute to understand the zooming tools and shortcuts as well as a few other techniques like nudging regions, hiding tracks, and the floating toolbox to quickly switch your tool.

Playback Position

What's more fundamental in a DAW than being able to control where playback starts? The Spacebar or the play button in the Transport bar enable playback. When you want to start playback at a specific location, you have a few options in Logic. Single-clicking in the lower half of the bar ruler will take you where you want to go; clicking again will engage the transport.

However, if you have a cycle set in your bar ruler, you might get thrown off that the playhead goes to the cycle start (left locator) when you press the Spacebar. The trick here is to use your Marquee tool.

Click into the Arrange workspace where you want to start playback, and the tool will make a playback position marker that appears as a white vertical line that is the height of a single track in the workspace grid. This playback position will take priority over the cycle selection in the bar ruler. Try it now—it's definitely very convenient.

Last but not least, use the key command Go To Position to type in an exact location. It defaults to the forward slash "/", but I use it so often and had such trouble remembering that keystroke that I reassigned it to is the G key, for "Go To Position." You'll find it included in appendix A, "Dot's Favorite Key Commands."

Zooming Shortcuts

- **Control + Option modifier key combination:** Holding down a combination of the Control + Option modifier keys will activate the Zoom tool. Whatever section of the Arrange workspace you now drag across with the Zoom tool will enlarge to fill the screen. Click into the empty space of the Arrange workspace while still holding the two modifier keys (Ctrl + Option), and the zoom scale reverts to the previous zoom level. This is the preferred zoom method for myself as well as many longtime Logic users. It may seem awkward until you get the hang of this classic Logic zooming technique. The Pointer turns into a magnifying glass, representing the Zoom tool when you hold down Ctrl + Option. With the two keys held down, drag across the area you want to enlarge in the Arrange window. You will start to have a feel for exactly how big an area to select to achieve the right zoom scale. What's nice about this technique is that you are not limited to specific zoom levels (unlike with other DAWs) but can control exactly the desired scale.
- **Drag down from the bar ruler with playhead:** This is a newer zoom technique that some users may prefer. Simply drag down from the bar ruler into the Arrange area with your Pointer tool to zoom in (drag up to zoom out)—the Pointer tool turns into the Zoomer tool as you drag.

Here are a few key commands to use for zooming. Write them down, practice, and commit to memory whichever ones feel useful to your workflow.

- **Zoom to Fit Selection or All Content:** Highlight an area, and then press this key command, assigned to Z (for "zoom").

The next three zooming key commands have no default assignment but are very useful, so you may want to make assignments that feel logical and easy to remember.

- **Zoom to Fit All Contents:** Everything in the Arrange window will be fit into view (recommended assignment is Shift + Z).
- **Zoom Horizontal In and Out:** Recommended assignment is Ctrl + Left and Right Arrows, respectively.
- **Zoom Vertical In and Out:** Recommended assignment is Ctrl + Up and Down Arrows, respectively.

Setting Your Logic Project End Point in the Transport

Having the correct end point set in your project is practical for operations such as bouncing or exporting a track. There's no need for the function to be performed for what seems like days when the project is only 32 bars long!

There is a rectangular-shaped project end marker in the bar ruler that you can drag to set the end point.

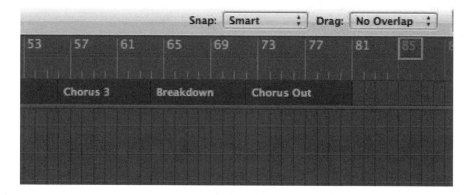

Figure 3.8: Project end point marker in the bar ruler

However, there is another method in the transport for setting the project end point that you may find easier for being precise. Click on the numerical value in the bottom row of the transport beneath the tempo, and type in the desired value for your project end point. You can watch the project end marker up in the bar ruler jump to the designated location.

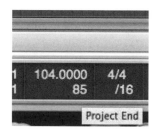

Figure 3.9: Setting the project end point in the transport

Drag by the Tick, the Smallest Nudge Value

To drag or nudge a region or note event by a tick, hold down the Control + Shift keys. You need to perform this operation in the correct sequence, or it won't work—highlight the region first, and then hold down the two modifier keys.

The value of the tick (1/3,840th of a beat) didn't come out of thin air. The standard for hardware sequencers, 960 PPQ (Pulses per Quarter Note), became the standard for hardware sequencers after the original 96 PPQ on early sequencers in the '80s.

Hiding Tracks You Don't Need to See

Another handy navigation tool is the ability to limit or hide what's in view in the Arrange window so that you can navigate quickly around the tracks and regions you need to focus on.

There are two steps to hiding tracks. First, enable the Hide button in the toolbar right above the track list in the Arrange window. The icon on the Hide button is the letter "H." When selected, it glows a bright lime green, and an H button appears on all of the track faders in the track list to the left of the Record Enable button.

Figure 3.10: Track hide in toolbar

Now, click on the Hide button of each track that you don't want in view. The track can be muted or unmuted, so it will play back even while hidden.

Once all the tracks are identified, press the H button again in the toolbar, and all the selected tracks will be removed from view in the Arrange window. The Hide button now turns orange, indicating that there are hidden tracks. The Hide button is a toggle. Press it again and the hidden tracks will be back in view.

This is extremely handy if you don't need to see a group of tracks that may not be part of the final arrangement but you don't want to delete them. Or, maybe you just want to focus on one group of tracks, like the vocals or drums, in the Arrange area— especially when it's a large project. While you're mixing all 24 vocal tracks, you may not want your visual focus to be distracted by all the orchestral, synth, or drum parts. This is a particularly great technique for a mix engineer who might get distracted by seeing a bunch of tracks in an unfamiliar session. It can really help the focusing process, especially if you're new to Logic.

Be careful—it's easy to forget about tracks you've hidden and get confused looking at your Logic project. The orange glow on the Hide button is your reminder that there are hidden tracks. However, you may still find yourself wondering what on earth you're hearing but not seeing. You'll smile when you remember it's that group of tracks you hid last week but didn't mute.

If they are tracks that are outtakes for your session but you're not ready to commit to deleting, you will likely want them muted and hidden. You have two techniques for muting. You can either throw the tracks into a group (see the section "Creating Track Groups," in chapter 7), mute any single track in the group, and the rest will update to a mute status, or you can drag across their mute switches in the track list. Trust me, it's fast!

The Floating Toolbox with the Escape Key

The Escape key was the original way to access tools in Logic. It is still a very slick solution and often the most convenient alternative for tool switching.

When you press the Escape key, a floating toolbox appears wherever your Pointer tool is. This allows you to select another tool as your primary tool, without having to move your eye from its current focal point and lose concentration—this toolbox comes to you! When you're working on a large monitor or dual monitors, that is especially convenient.

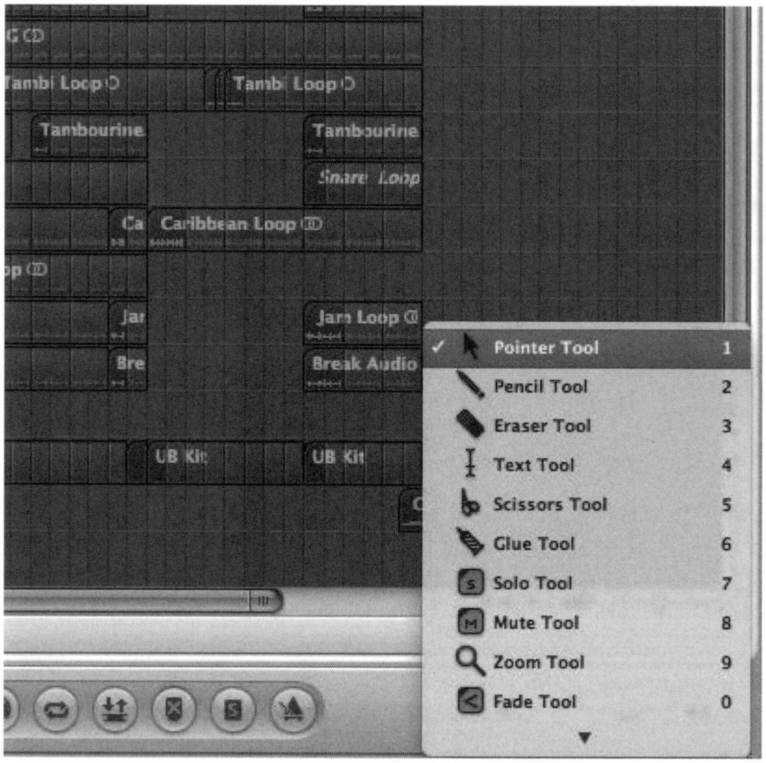

Figure 3.11: Floating toolbox via the Escape key

Navigation Tips for Pro Tools Users

Here are some basic navigation key commands to assign, particularly for users who are used to working in Pro Tools:

- Leave the Spacebar set as "Play."
- Set the key command Ctrl + Spacebar to "Play from Selection."
- Set the key command Option + Spacebar to "Go To Selection Start."
- Set the 0 (zero) key to "Play or Stop and Go To Last Locate Position."
- Set the key command Shift + R to "Set Locators by Regions/Events/Marquee."

Editing at Maximum Speed

Editing not just MIDI but audio in Logic is easy and fast when you know how. That means you have to invest a little time in familiarizing yourself with the relevant Preferences for Logic's editing tools and view options, the Snap and Drag modes in the Arrange window, and other editing basics like scrubbing and adjusting the anchor point of an audio region. This next section has many of the finer points of Logic editing I've been asked about so often that you will thank yourself for making time to investigate.

Very Important Editing Preferences

There are a lot of great preferences in the editing preferences dialog box and how you assign them depends on your taste. From Preferences in the toolbar, select General and then Editing (Preferences > General > Editing).

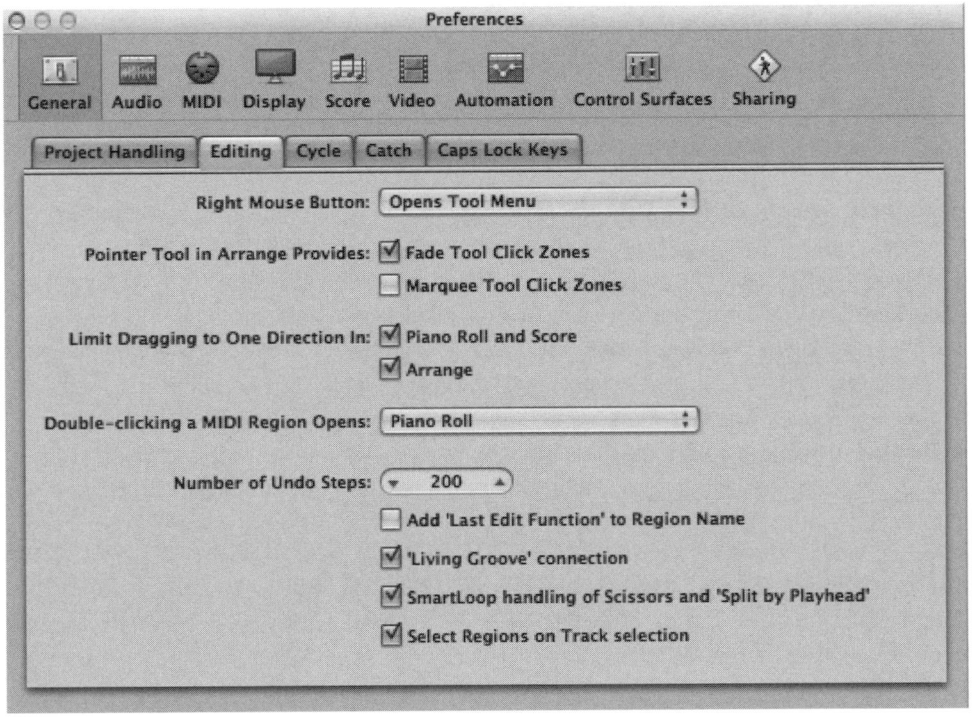

Figure 3.12: Editing preferences

- **Right Mouse Button:** Assign your mouse right-click to a third tool. This sort of navigation is generally considered convenient by PC users.
- **Pointer Tool in Arrange Provides:** Fade Tool and Marquee Tool Click Zones can be introduced to the Pointer tool's functionality. I recommend experimenting here to see if they work for you. The Fade Tool Click Zones assignment is very slick and allows you to simply swipe across the upper right or left of a region to create a fade. With the Marquee Tool Click Zones enabled, your Pointer tool will always switch to the Marquee tool when clicking in the lower half of a region.

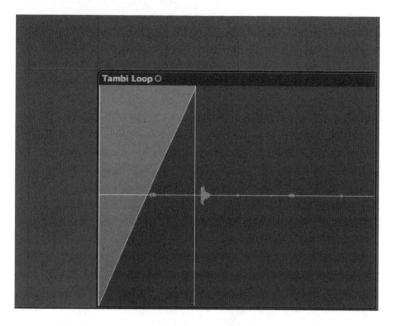

Figure 3.13: Fade Tool Click Zones

- **Limit Dragging to One Direction In:** You may find this very valuable to enabled in the Arrange window as well as in the Score and Piano Roll editors. Generally when moving regions around, you will be moving them either forward or backward in the timeline and won't want them to slip to the track below or above. Similarly, if I'm moving data up or down to another track, I won't want it to move forward or back in the timeline. This preference is a personal favorite—in fact, it's essential. It's one of the first things I enable when I sit down at someone else's Logic system.
- **Double-Clicking a MIDI region opens:** You may want to leave this on Piano Roll. If you're a composer or more traditional musician, you may prefer the Score or Event List to open here.

Edit Grid Modes: Snap, Drag, and Shuffle

This feature throws off a lot of Pro Tools users, so read carefully and then explore on your own. The Edit modes in the upper right corner of the Arrange window determine how regions will behave when you move them around, especially if you move them on top of one another.

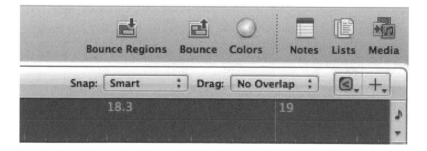

Figure 3.14: Snap and Drag modes

The Drag modes refer to the behavior of regions in the Arrange window. The default mode is Overlap, while No Overlap mode most resembles the behavior in Pro Tools. The Snap modes determine the division that Logic regions snap to when editing, whether Bar, Beat, Division, Tick (1/3,840th of a beat), or the default on top, which is Smart Snap and is dependent on your zoom level. It is the best choice most of the time, unless you are performing a specific edit task requiring that regions move by a designated amount, such as a beat or a bar.

Power Tip: No Overlap Mode as Default (Drag menu)

I recommend switching to No Overlap in the Drag modes. This is the standard mode in Pro Tools and forces regions to replace each other when one is placed on top of the other. When you are editing audio, any region underneath another audio file will be eliminated.

Shuffle Right and Shuffle Left are self-explanatory. When enabled, regions will behave like magnets, butting up to the region to the right or left, depending on whether Shuffle Right or Shuffle Left is selected.

Fades and Crossfades

Logic is straightforward and comprehensive when it comes to drawing fades on audio regions or crossfades between them.

The Fade Tool

The Fade tool can be accessed from the Tool menu in the upper right of Arrange window or from the floating toolbox opened with the Escape key. With the Fade tool, you can draw on either side of an audio region, and then adjust the settings in the Region Parameter box in the upper left of the Arrange window. The Fade tool turns into the shape of a crosshair-style tool when you grab the region corner. If you find yourself not being able to draw in a fade, you're probably not grabbing on the corner of the region properly, so move your Fade tool around slightly until you find the sweet spot and the tool icon switches to the crosshair.

Figure 3.15: The Fade tool

Crossfades

To clean up edit points, you can apply a crossfade by dragging the Crossfade tool over the intersection of two regions. Then, hold down the Control key and adjust the curve of the fade. If you want to make precise changes to the crossfade range, you can do that in the Playback parameters. Highlight multiple regions at once to apply crossfades simultaneously.

Another option is to enable the preference for automatic crossfades.

Automatic Crossfades (Drag menu)

The X-Fade mode creates automatic crossfades between regions, which can be pretty convenient. This will create an automatic crossfade when two regions overlap as the result of an edit.

Figure 3.16: X-Fade mode

Speed Fades

Speed Fades are drawn on audio files like traditional fades. I first mentioned this creative technique in my previous book, *The Power in Logic Pro*, in chapter 9's "DJ and Electronic Music Tricks," but engineers appreciate this tool so much that it is worth repeating here.

Speed Fades introduce a ramp up or down in tempo within an audio region and the *shwooshing* pitched artifacts of turntable tricks to accent the buildup of a selection. They are drawn onto the corner of an audio region, like traditional fades.

Steps to Create a Speed Fade

- Highlight the target region in the Arrange window.
- In the Region Parameter box, select Speed Up from the menu under Fade In or Speed Down from the menu under Fade Out.
- Directly next to the type of fade selected, adjust the numeric value for the amount.
- As you increase the value, you will see a more dramatic slope to the fade that will be visible in orange on the audio file.
- Adjust the curve with the parameter beneath, labeled Curve. Try it with extreme values!

Spotting with the Anchor Point

Spotting with the anchor point allows you to place a specific MIDI event (that is, a sound effect in the EXS24, or an audio event) at an exact frame of video or SMPTE location. As long as you can see the frame you want to match, you can move the MIDI or audio event to that frame.

- Assign a key command for Create Marker Without Rounding (I use the "=" (equals) key). Note: This key command will not round the marker to the closest bar.

- Place a few markers at unrounded locations, at the exact SMPTE position of frames where you want a musical event to occur.
- Open a SMPTE-view transport (in the upper right of the Arrange window, click on the music note).
- Drag on SMPTE values to select precise movie locations.
- Open an EXS24 instrument. I've created a custom kit of sound effects that comes in quite handy.
- Place a sound effect at approximate locations to markers—don't try to land exactly.
- Set the key command for Pickup Clock (Ctrl + P).
- Move the playhead to the first marker.
- Select/highlight the first MIDI event in the Score, Matrix, or Event list.
- Press the Pickup Clock (Ctrl + P) key command, and the MIDI event will jump to the song position.

(Note: The graphics in the Arrange window of the MIDI data won't redraw to the new location until you click off the MIDI data.)

Power Tip: Enabling SMPTE View in the Bar Ruler

If you look under any of the main menus in the Arrange window, you will not find the option to view SMPTE time in the bar ruler. The introduction of SMPTE time to the bar ruler is achieved by clicking on the small note or clock icon at the upper right edge of the ruler. This opens a menu of alternate bar and (SMPTE) time display settings. Here you can choose between time and bar linear views.

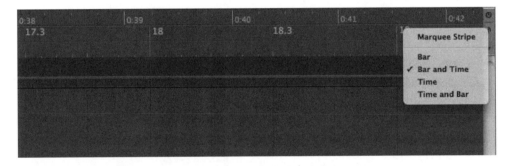

Figure 3.17: Enabling SMPTE view in the bar ruler

Special Situation: Anchors

When you want a part of the audio file (or sound effect)—other than the beginning—to lock to a SMPTE frame (for example, the final bang at the end of a falling or otherwise crashing object), you can take advantage of the file's anchor point.

- Open the sample editor on the audio file/sound effect.
- Move the black triangle underneath the waveform labeled "Anchor" to the point in the audio file where you want to lock to the SMPTE address in the Arrange window.
- Use the Pickup Clock key command introduced above.

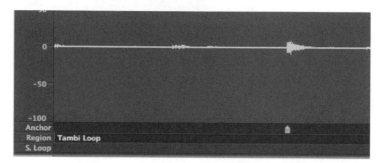

Figure 3.18: The anchor point of an audio file

Spotting in the Audio Window (not the Audio Bin)

This can be confusing at first, but easy when you know how. There are two different pathways to your Audio Bin. There is the Audio Bin in the Media section of the Arrange window, in the same section where you access Apple Loops and channel strip settings. This is generally your "go to" bin for accessing the audio files of your project. For special tasks like spotting, however, there is also a separate Audio Bin window (Window > Audio Bin).

- In the upper right of the Arrange window, switch the bar ruler view to the SMPTE time ruler with the small note icon or clock icon.
- Use the Go to Position key command (default "/") to mouse/scrub to SMPTE value.
- Select an audio track in the Arrange window.
- In the Audio window (Arrange > Window > Audio), Command-click on the audio region name and the region will jump to that SMPTE location/Song Position in the Arrange window.
- The song will jump to the end of the region, so another sound effect or audio file can be placed directly adjacent to the first.

Scrubbing Audio

Scrubbing allows you to hear audio (and MIDI) regions directly on the playhead position so you can locate a particular event for editing purposes.

To scrub audio (or MIDI) events, do the following:

- Set the zoom level for the best view of the selection to scrub. See the section "Zooming Shortcuts," earlier in this chapter.
- Click on the Pause button in the Transport bar.
- Grab the playhead in the Arrange area or bar ruler and move it back and forth over the selection, or use the Scrub Rewind and Scrub Forward key commands (no default assignments).

Keep in mind that if no regions are selected, all regions will be scrubbed. Also, the Mute and Solo track status has an effect on what you hear when scrubbing to allow for isolating the scrubbed selection.

Power Tip: Scrubbing MIDI Events

To scrub MIDI events, turn on File > Project Settings > MIDI > General > Scrubbing with Audio in Arrange. If this setting is selected, all MIDI regions are always scrubbed, regardless of the selection status.

Chapter 4

QUICK SWIPE COPING

Basic Terminology of the Take Folder

If you are an engineer who is familiar with Pro Tools playlists, the idea of *comping*—compiling a master track from the best parts of different performances—is quite familiar. While it may be a bit challenging adapting to the Logic workflow at first, you hopefully will come to appreciate the visual detail offered by Logic's take folders and quick swipe comping. You are able to see all of your takes at the same time!

What the Take Folder Is

The take folder (which was introduced in the section "Takes Recording and the Take Folder," in chapter 2) is automatically created when you record over an existing audio region. A "take" is essentially an audio recording. Multiple takes can be combined into the composite track using the Quick Swipe Comping feature, allowing you to select the best parts from all the takes by simply swiping across the desired area of a take region.

Click on the disclosure triangle in the upper left of an audio track to open and close the take folder and otherwise view and edit the contents of the folder.

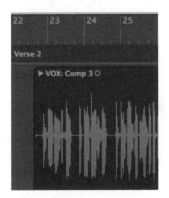

Figure 4.1: The disclosure triangle
to view takes

Inside the take folder are the take lanes. When the take folder is revealed, it looks as though is consists of multiple audio tracks, but in actuality they are all recordings contained within one single audio track in the Arrange window.

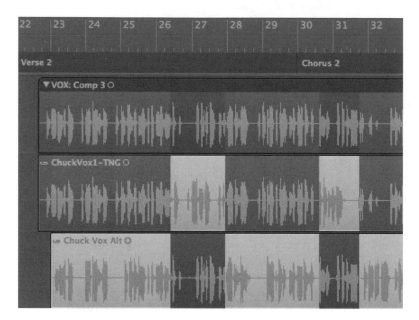

Figure 4.2: Take lanes

The Comp Track

The top lane inside a take folder is the composite or "comp" track. This is the master take combining the best parts you've selected from all the individual takes. You can watch it update each time you swipe across an area of one of the take lanes beneath with the Pointer or the Pencil tool.

Removing Areas of the Comp Track

When you select a section of a take, Logic automatically deselects the same section in another take region. If you Shift-click on a take region section, it is simply removed and there will be silence during that passage of time. Shift-clicking again on the same take region area will act as a toggle and restore that section to the comp.

Naming a Comp, Creating Another One

You can name the comp by clicking on the disclosure triangle on the right side of the take folder and selecting Rename Comp. In fact, there are a ton of operations that can be performed from this menu, such as creating a new comp so you can compare different versions. All these comping tasks are covered in the next section of this chapter.

Figure 4.3: The comp track in the take folder

Defining the Take Selection

You can swipe across an area of a take with the Pointer or Pencil tool to add it to the master comp track above.

A great trick is to click into another take above or below the selected area to replace that piece of the timeline with a selection from a different take.

Extend a take region section by dragging the start point to the left or the end point to the right. Shift-drag the left or right corner of a region of a take to introduce the bracket-shaped Pointer tool, which allows for empty space or silence in the comp.

Everything You Can Do in a Take Folder

On the upper right of the take folder is the Take Folder menu with a whole host of functions that you can perform on your comp and take folder. You should make time to experiment with the options so that you choose the right one for the given situation. You'll find that the options are quite comprehensive with subtle but useful variations, including the following:

- Saving and deleting takes and comps
- Naming takes or comps
- Creating new comps
- Copying comps
- Unpacking takes to individual audio tracks
- Exporting takes to leave the originals intact
- Flattening and merging take folders into independent audio regions to replace the take folder

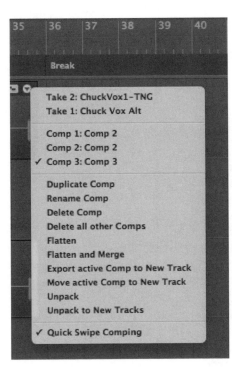

Figure 4.4: The Take Folder menu

The Edit Modes of Comping

There are two editing modes available within take folders. One is specifically for all the comping moves introduced in this chapter, and the other is for performing general Logic editing functions. The indication for these modes is admittedly subtle.

1. **Quick Swipe Comping mode enabled:** You can freely create and edit comps. The icon in the upper right has a white background when the comping mode is enabled.

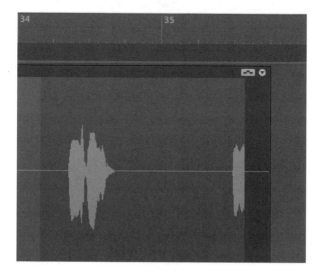

Figure 4.5: Quick Swipe Comping enabled

2. **Quick Swipe Comping mode disabled:** You can perform any familiar Logic editing operations—for example, cut, edit, and drag regions within a take folder. This is the same as editing regular audio regions in the Arrange window. The icon in the upper right has a dark background when the comping mode is disabled.

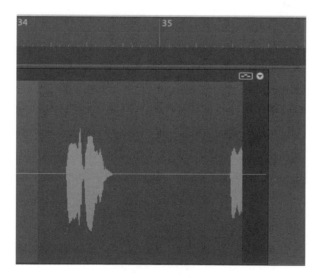

Figure 4.6: Quick Swipe Comping disabled and Logic editing available

Power Tip: Modifying a Closed Take Folder

When the take folder is closed and the individual takes are no longer visible, you can still select between various takes by Control-clicking on a take region. A pop-up menu with the various takes is visible where you can highlight a take to select it.

Figure 4.7: Modifying a closed take folder

Cool Trick: Packing Regions into Take Folders

Packing regions into take folders can be a useful technique for an engineer when there were multiple performances recorded but not into a take folder, possibly in another application, that you now want to create a comp track with. Packing regions into a take folder is performed from the Region menu in the Arrange local menu bar (Region > Folder > Pack Take Folder). The default key command is Control + Command + F. The newly created take folder will play back from the channel strip of the topmost track. A bit of fine print to be aware of—this may affect playback if the regions were on differing channel strips.

When this gets creative (and really belongs in the first Quick Pro book in this series on remixing and songwriting, *The Power in Logic Pro*) is that you can pack drum loops into a take folder and cut between them for a cool breakbeat effect.

Figure 4.8: Packing regions into a take folder

Chapter 5

FLEX AUDIO: THE FLEX TOOL AND AUDIO QUANTIZING

All About Flex Audio ("elastic audio")

Flex Audio is Logic's interpretation of "elastic audio," which makes it painless to adjust the timing, tempo, and rhythm of your audio tracks. After enabling Flex view in the toolbar and selecting an algorithm to analyze the transients on an audio track, you are able to make infinite changes to the timing of a beat or the phrasing and musical inflection of a vocal track. When Flex mode is enabled, there is a white halo around the icon in the toolbar.

Figure 5.1: Flex mode in the toolbar

Enabling Flex Mode

Enabling Flex mode in the toolbar opens up this universe of elastic time. Click on the Hide/Show Flex View tool icon. If it's not in view, Control-click in the toolbar area to customize the toolbar. A sheet of tools is revealed that you can drag into the toolbar area, which is introduced in the section "Super Fast Tour of the Logic Workspace," in chapter 1.

Once Flex mode is enabled, you'll find a menu of modes to choose from inside the track header on the track list for each audio track. The default view is "Off." Click into that area of the track header, and you'll find a menu to choose which Flex mode (or algorithm) is appropriate for the task at hand. For beats, Slicing or Rhythmic is recommended. Once you select a mode, the transients are detected on that track and are visible as gray lines in the waveform. Keep in mind that the flex mode is enabled per track, not per individual region.

Flex editing is entirely nondestructive, and you can enable and disable it for an individual region at any time in the Region Parameter box.

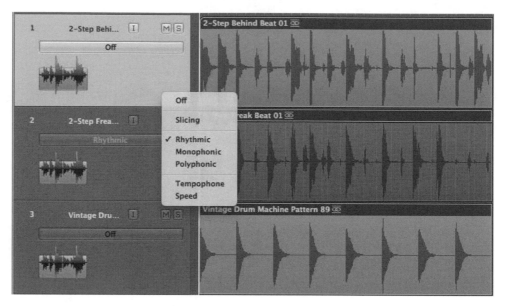

Figure 5.2: Selecting your Flex mode on a track

Flex Markers Are for Editing

The flex markers are the vertical orange lines with little handles at the top. These are the edit points that can be dragged forward and backward in time to expand or compress the audio that came before and change your musical phrasing. Specifically, flex markers determine the boundaries of your Flex edits. The visual feedback in Flex view is fantastic. Color-coding helps you see at a glance what portions of the audio are getting affected and how. Green indicates time compression and red reveals any time expansion.

Figure 5.3: Enabling flex per region

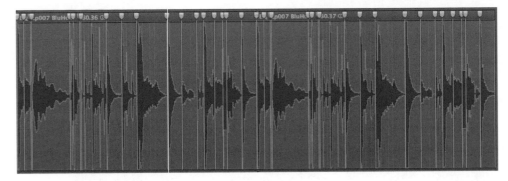

Figure 5.4: Flex markers and Flex Time color-coding

To add a new flex marker, click in the upper half of the waveform, and a flex marker will be created at the clicked position. Moving a flex marker to the left time-compresses the preceding audio material, and moving it to the right will time-expand the preceding audio material from any preceding flex marker up to the moved marker. Flex markers can be dragged either at the white line over the waveform or on the orange handle above. To delete a flex marker, simply double-click on it.

Quantizing and Regrooving Your Audio
Once transients are detected on a track, the same quantize menu in the Region Parameter box is available to audio as with MIDI. Simply select the quantize value and swing percentage as you would for a MIDI file, and experiment with the groove. Group-select tracks that have been flexed to assign the same quantize value and tighten the groove. See the section "Creating Track Groups" for the steps to creating track groups.

Figure 5.5: Quantizing audio in Logic after flexing

Cutting on Transients
Option-click on the region header in the Arrange workspace to access the Slice at Transient Markers feature. This can be performed without even enabling Flex mode on the track. Once you've sliced on the transients, there are infinite possibilities for editing out unwanted pieces of the region by muting or cutting between transients.

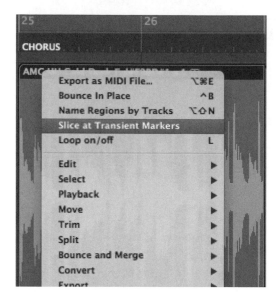

Figure 5.6: Slice at transient markers on region header

Power Tip: Flexing to Change Project Tempo or Remix Vocals

You can quickly change the tempo of a vocal track or even the entire project by flexing it first. Enable Flex mode in the toolbar, and then choose a mode to detect transients on all your tracks. Now, change the tempo in the Logic transport, and all the tracks will conform to the new tempo. It's best to perform the transient detection on tracks with the Logic tempo set to the same tempo as the audio files.

Instead of individually selecting tracks and detecting their transients, you can perform the transient detection on all tracks at once. Create a group containing all the tracks (see the section "Grouping Tracks," in chapter 7), then select an algorithm on any one of the track headers of a track within the group. The transients will be detected for your entire project at once, then you can make an efficient global tempo adjustment by simply changing the tempo in the transport.

The Sample Editor: Fine-Tuning Transient Detection (and other handy audio processing)

While sample-accurate editing can be performed in the Arrange window, the Sample Editor allows you to make a number of unique fine adjustments and processing alterations to your audio files that aren't possible directly in the Arrange window. It's accessed by double-clicking on an audio file in the Arrange window, or highlighting the file and selecting the tab for the Sample Editor at the bottom of the Arrange window.

At the top of the Sample Editor, you will find a set of local menus and buttons. Above the main waveform display is the waveform overview allowing you to see a complete representation of the entire audio file.

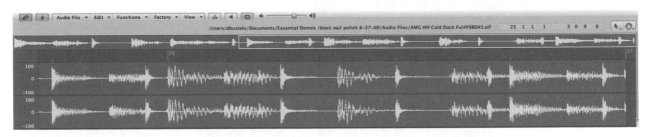

Figure 5.7: The Sample Editor's waveform display and overview

Keep in mind that audio processing in the Sample Editor is destructive. In other words, it is modifying the data of the original audio file as opposed to manipulating playback parameters. While there is undo in the Sample Editor, you may want to be safe and make a backup first (Audio File > Create Backup). The fine print here is that if you revert to the backup file, you cannot then return to the modified file. Examples of the audio processing that can be achieved in this editor include normalizing, changing gain, reversing, inverting phase, and pitch transposition or time expansion/compression processing in the Factory menu, one of the earliest Logic tools for manipulating audio.

Working with Transients

From the local audio file menu in the Sample Editor, choose Detect Transients (Audio File > Detect Transients). Use the Pencil tool to introduce a new transient. When the Transient Editing mode button is active, you can use the buttons to its right to increase or decrease the number of detected transients. Use the "+" and "-" buttons to increase or decrease the number of detected transients.

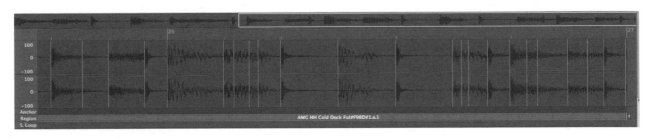

Figure 5.8: Transient editing in the Sample Editor

Deleting Transients

To delete a transient, use the Eraser tool or double-click directly on it with the Pencil tool. This is helpful when the transient detection has resulted in too many transient markers or the recording has a lot of background noise, pops, or clicks that the transient detection is identifying.

Power Tip: Soloing between Transients

To solo between transients, enable the speaker icon in the top row of the Sample Editor, select the Solo tool from the Tool menu or from the Escape key, and click between two transients. Cycle playback will begin between the transients, and the area will become shaded. You might want to assign this tool as your Command-click tool temporarily while you're working in this editor on cleaning up the transient detection.

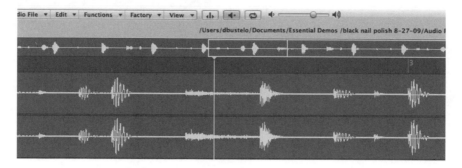

Figure 5.9: Speaker icon in the Sample Editor

Power Tip: Transient Editing Before Creating an EXS24 Sampler Track or Remixing a Vocal

Transient editing in the Sample Editor is highly recommended before attempting to create an EXS24 sampler instrument (Audio > Convert Regions to New Sampler Track). If transient editing is not performed, unwanted sample zones may be created in the new instrument.

Another common situation where it may be necessary to modify the automatic transient detection is if you are planning to adjust the timing of a vocal file for a remix. If too many transients are detected, it may result in unwanted glitches or vibratos when you change the tempo of the vocal.

Chapter 6

AFTER RECORDING THE BAND

When engineering a Logic project, you will surely win a lot of friends or at least capture the loyalty of the band and producer by having a full understanding of these next tools in Logic for manipulating the recordings of live musicians. Musicians who master these tools will be well on their way to independence in the studio with any live recording work.

Beat Mapping to Create a Tempo Map

While you can always conform your audio to Logic's tempo (see the section "Power Tip: Flexing to Change Project Tempo or Remix Vocals" in chapter 5), there are situations where it's better to have the bar and beat grid conformed to any subtle tempo changes of the audio—if, for example, you're working with audio that was recorded free-form without a click track, or maybe you have a long sample off of a record. In either case, you may want to maintain this original human feel. If the live musicians didn't play at a consistent tempo (whether intentionally or not), you can create a tempo map of the multiple tempos. This is easily achieved by using the Beat Mapping track.

The Global Tracks

The global tracks located under the bar ruler are—as the name implies—a set of tracks that affect parameters of all your tracks. They include Tempo, Signature, Chord, Transposition, Marker, Video (thumbnails), and Beat Mapping. Open the view of global tracks by clicking on the disclosure triangle to the left of the name "Global Tracks," on top of the track list.

Make sure that the Beat Mapping track is in view. If it isn't, Control-click on the global track's track header at the top of the track list to customize which global tracks are in view. Enable the checkbox for the Beat Mapping global track.

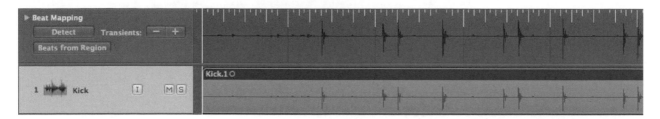

Figure 6.1: The Beat Mapping track in the global tracks

Next, select the kick track performed by the live drummer. Ideally, move the track up by dragging on its track header so that it's adjacent to the global track. This will make it easier to see what you're doing.

Detecting Transients on the Beat Mapping Track

With the kick track highlighted, select Detect in the Beat Mapping track to detect the tempo. Now you will see the transients that have been identified in the kick track displayed in the global track. The transients are the white vertical lines that appear in the lower half of the Beat Mapping track.

Figure 6.2: Detect transients

Creating the Beat Map

The top half of the Beat Mapping track has the constant grid of Logic's bar ruler. Zoom in tight so you can look closely as you perform the next step. Listen to the kick line and drag the downbeat of a bar marking to the actual transient. The exact tempo will be created down to fractions of a beat, all the way to four decimal points. The tempo will be displayed in the Tempo track, also in the global tracks.

You can check your work by creating 2-bar cycles anywhere and enabling the metronome in the Transport area. Any kick that falls on the "1" will land right on Logic's downbeat in time with the click each time.

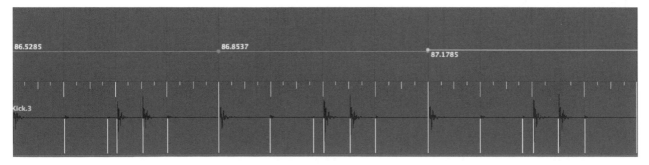

Figure 6.3: Beat Mapping on the transients

Power Tip: SMPTE Lock Audio Before Editing

Select all tracks, and then Control-click on an individual region to view the contextual menu to SMPTE lock to time. This will ensure that your audio regions don't move if you change tempo. Or from the Region menu, select Lock SMPTE position.

Region ▾	MIDI ▾	Audio ▾	View ▾	
Add to Apple Loops Library...				
Set Locators by Regions				=
Folder				▶
Loops				▶
Split				▶
Merge				▶
Bounce Regions in Place				^B
Cut/Insert Time				▶
Remove Overlaps				–
Trim Region End to Next Region				⇧-
Shuffle Regions Left within Selection				⌥[
Shuffle Regions Right within Selection				⌥]
Trim Regions to Fill within Locators				⌥-
Unlock SMPTE Position				⌘‡
Lock SMPTE Position				⌘‡
Repeat Regions...				⌘R
Move Selected Regions to Selected Track				⇧⌘T
Name Regions by Tracks/Channel Strips				⌥⇧N
Color Regions by Channel Strips/Instruments				⌥⇧C

Figure 6.4: SMPTE-lock position

The Tempo List

You can view and edit the various tempo changes in a list view from the Options menu in the Arrange window (Options > Tempo > Open Tempo List).

Power Tip: Waveform Zoom Button

This was introduced in the section "Super Fast Tour of the Logic Workspace," in chapter 2, but is worth repeating here because it directly impacts the beat mapping workflow. Directly beneath the Arrange workspace and to the right of the left/right scrollbar is the Waveform Zoom button to adjust the scale of the waveform on a track. The icon for it is a waveform.

Click on the icon and a transparent vertical slider pops up. Drag up on the slider, and the waveform increases in size making it easier to view the peaks for editing; drag down and the waveform decreases in scale. This same Waveform Zoom button can be used to visually resize the waveform here in the Beat Mapping track.

Drum Replacement ("Sound Replacement")

Drum Replacement is a great example of a tool in Logic Pro that helps musicians achieve professionally engineered results on their own. Logic's Drum Replacement employs a technique used for years by audio engineers and simplifies the process down to a few steps. For example, imagine that you didn't get the best sonic recording of a drummer's snare, although you really like the part the drummer played. Drum Replacement fixes this up pretty fast.

The How-To of Logic's Drum Replacement

- Simply click on Drum Replacement/Doubling from the local Track menu.
- Logic will automatically create an EXS24 sampler instrument on a new track, detect the drum hits in the original audio track, and create a MIDI performance out of the drum hits on the EXS track.
- After Logic creates an EXS24 instrument, it immediately opens the Library, giving you choices for sounds to replace or double the snare (Track > Drum Replacement/Doubling).

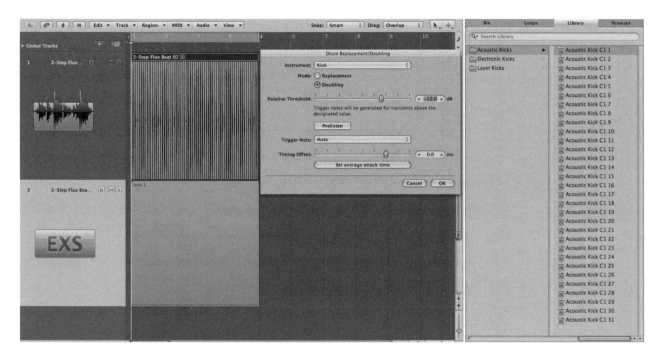

Figure 6.5: Drum Replacement with EXS24 in Track menu

- In the Drum Replacement/Doubling window that opens, you can tell Logic a little bit about what you want to do with the sound. You can select the type of sound you want to replace (for example, a kick or snare) and the Library will update automatically to bring that category of drum sounds into view.
- Here, you can also choose between Replacement or Doubling. Choose Replacement for now if you are trying this out.
- Next you need to choose the Relative Threshold—how sensitive Logic should be when determining which hits in the audio file it should create note triggers for. The ideal setting will depend on the relative level of the recorded drum, how well it is isolated from other signal sources, and whether it's experiencing any bleed from other instruments.
- Click on the Prelisten button to determine if any adjustments should be made to the Relative Threshold or the replacement sound itself. Once the threshold setting is satisfactory, you can experiment with a few options for a new snare sound.
- In most cases, you will want to leave the Trigger Note setting on Auto. The defaults are C1 for the Kick, D1 for the Snare, and A1 for the Tom.

- Clicking on OK now will commit the changes made and mute the previous snare recording because you chose Replace instead of Double.

Audio to Score in Sample Editor

The technique of Audio to Score was available for years in Logic. It was quite popular with advanced Logic users, but wasn't as obvious to the new user. The Audio to Score feature in the Sample Editor under Factory is still available to replace or just augment kicks, fatten up a snare or other drum parts.

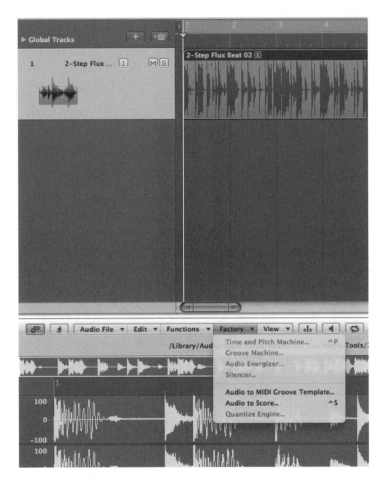

Figure 6.6: Audio to Score in the Sample Editor's Factory

Audio to Score works the same way that Drum Replacement/Doubling does as far as creating MIDI notes from any selected audio file, but it doesn't automatically open a dialog box to choose what type of drum you're replacing on an EXS24 sample instrument track. You need to manually open a new software instrument track with the EXS24, Ultrabeat, or another favorite drum instrument. Take a live snare track and open the Audio to Score Editor. It immediately analyzes the whole audio performance. Some of it you may not want—maybe you just want to catch the backbeats and the important hits, not all the little ghosting of a real snare playing. So push the granulation and the velocity threshold up to approximately 21, then process, and there is your MIDI performance.

You can force all the hits to the same pitch to quickly get rid of any sloppy notes and bring up all their velocities. In the Arrange window, you will see the original snare and the new MIDI performance right below it. Open Ultrabeat and shop for the right snare sound by using one of the Drum Bank kits, such as the Acoustic Snare bank. This way, you can just transpose pitch in the Region Parameter box to audition different snares.

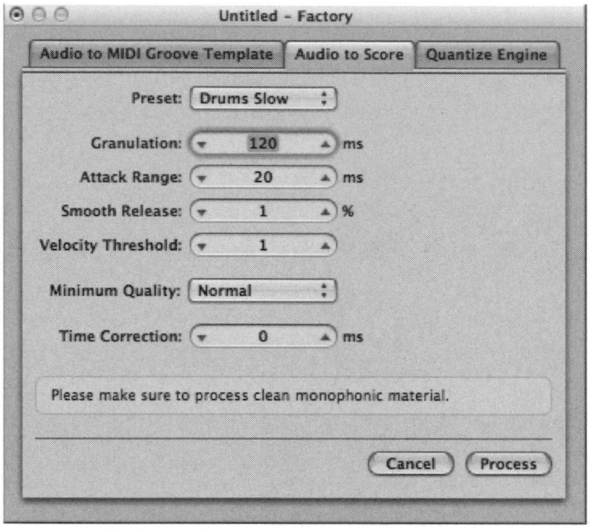

Figure 6.7: The Audio to Score window

Time-Stretching

Logic provides a complete set of tools and techniques for time-stretching audio, depending on the task at hand, whether you're working with an entire song file or just a few bars of music. Give yourself time to experiment with each one in this next section so you'll be prepared for any creative or problem-solving situation.

BPM Plug-In and Tap Tempo to Find Tempo

Locking audio files to the project tempo is key to any remixing work. There are many different techniques to achieve this in Logic, depending on the situation. The BPM plug-in is great for getting a quick readout of the tempo of a long audio file (for example, a song someone sent you or one you dragged in from iTunes).

The BPM plug-in is located in the Metering subfolder of Logic plug-ins. Just insert it on the audio track, start playback, and then give it a few seconds to read the file's tempo. You'll be surprised at how accurate it is when you switch Logic's tempo to the beats per minute that the plug-in finds, and turn on the click in the transport.

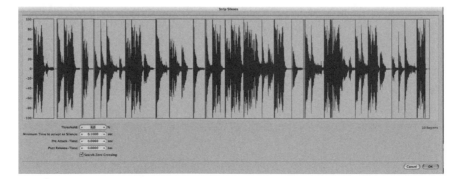

Figure 6.8: BPM Plug-In to find tempo

Tap Tempo is a common technique used in computer-based music software and some drum machines to be able to manually tap out a tempo and have the sequencer clock update to that tempo. Tap Tempo in Logic has a few "gotchas" to be aware of. For example, the Transport must be stopped to tap in the tempo. This means that the audio file has to be playing on another machine or in another app, like iTunes. Let's at least take a look at how it works, since it's such a popular question.

Here is the setup for how to use Tap Tempo in Logic:

- Choose File > Project Settings > Synchronization > Turn Sync mode to "Manual."
- Be sure that the checkbox beneath Sync mode, "Auto enable external sync," is checked.
- The bar ruler will turn blue.
- Select a software instrument, and then tap at least four times with the Tap Tempo key command (the default is Shift + T).
- With Auto Sync enabled, Logic will jump into Manual sync mode after tapping the Tap Tempo key command four times.
- Logic's tempo in the transport will update accordingly.

Adjusting Logic's Tempo to the Beat (or vocal)

Here's the scenario: You have an audio sample of a beat, and you want to conform Logic's tempo to the sample. Sometimes you find a beat and realize that what you started will actually sound better at the new tempo of imported audio.

- First make sure that the sample is perfectly looping (whether 2, 4, 8 bars, and so on) and placed on a downbeat in Logic. To do this, highlight the audio file in the Arrange area, select the Set Locators tool in the toolbar, and start playback.
- Logic will cycle the highlighted region. When it comes back around to the downbeat, listen for any hiccups in the beat (for example, hearing two kicks flamming or the downbeat kick dropping too soon).
- If necessary, create a perfect audio loop in the Arrange window with the Zoom and Marquee tools for cutting.
- If you are starting with a long audio file (for example, a whole record), use the Marquee tool to make loose cuts to bring the file size down closer to the target length of the loop, whether two or four bars.
- Zoom in on the audio file while the audio is looping, with the Set Locators tool enabled in the toolbar and the region highlighted.
- Once the audio sample is perfectly looping, set the bar ruler cycle length to that same number of bars as the loop, whether 1, 2, 4, 8 etc., and so on. The bar ruler will not match region length. For example, if it's a 4-bar loop, highlight four bars in Logic's bar ruler.
- From the Options menu, go to Tempo > Adjust Tempo Using Region Length and Locators.
- Logic's tempo will update to conform to the tempo of the audio loop.

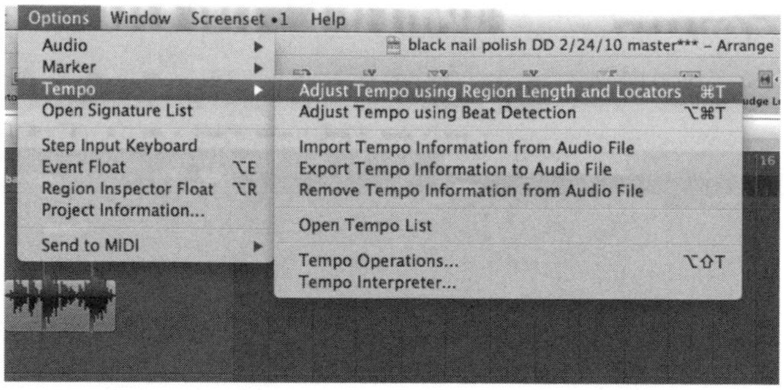

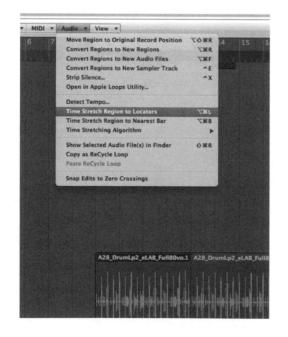

Figure 6.10: Setting Logic's tempo to a sampled loop

You have now changed Logic's tempo to conform to the tempo of the audio file! All you had to do was let Logic know how many bars the drum loop should equal in Logic.

Time-Stretching Audio to Logic's Tempo

More often the goal is the reverse—to lock an audio file or sampled loop to Logic's tempo. The audio source may be from a record, or a sample library, or one you recorded in your own studio. It's a common production technique to adjust the loop from its original tempo. This will change the tempo of the audio file and its length, but not its pitch. Once again, it starts with a trimmed audio file that is perfectly looping that you want to conform to Logic's tempo.

Below are the steps to use, once you have a trimmed, perfect loop.

- Highlight the region.
- In the bar ruler, select however many bars match the number of bars of the loop. If it is a 2-bar loop, select two bars in the bar ruler.
- In the local audio menu, select Time Stretch Region to Locators.
- Watch as the imported audio loop "shrinks" to perfectly fit the 2-bar length selected in the bar ruler.

Figure 6.11: Time-stretching the loop to Logic's tempo

In this same local audio menu, you will find different time-stretching algorithms to experiment with. The default, Universal, is a good place to start. The Legacy Algorithms are useful for different types of material, such as Monophonic or Pads, for the situations that the names imply.

Another technique regarding imported beats is if you find you prefer the tempo of the audio you dragged in and decide you want to conform your Logic project to its tempo. The process starts out the same as when you want to conform an audio file to Logic's tempo. Be sure that the audio loop is perfectly looping and starting on a downbeat in Logic, highlight it, then highlight the number of bars in the bar rule to match (for example, if it's a 4-bar loop, highlight four bars in Logic's bar ruler, even though that will be a different length than the length of the loop).

Option-Drag to Time-Stretch Audio

Logic also now allows you to time-stretch or time-compress an audio region directly in the Arrange area without changing its pitch. This technique was available for years for MIDI data. Simply Option-drag the end point of the region to where you want it to end, and the speed of the beat will be adjusted. For example, if the beat was one bar in duration, drag it to where one bar is defined in Logic by the bar ruler.

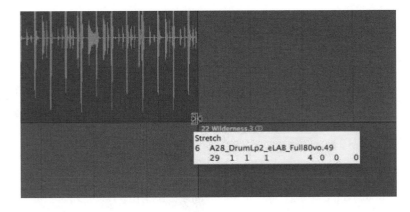

Figure 6.12: Option-drag to time-compress or time-stretch

Power Tip: Time-Stretching with Snap to Absolute Value

Time-stretching with the Option-drag technique works especially well with the Snap to Absolute Value option in the Snap menu. The Snap menu is located in the upper right of the Arrange window. Snapping to absolute value constrains your edits to the nearest defined snap point as defined in this menu (for example, Beat, Bar, and so on).

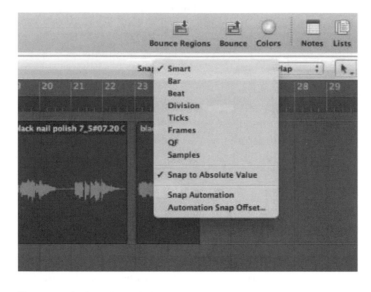

Figure 6.13: Snap to Absolute Value

Strip Silence

While the ability to flex audio to detect transients and then quantize it in the Region Parameter box eliminates some of the original use of Logic's Strip Silence window. However, engineers will still find it helpful for cleaning up a live performance, maybe removing pops and clicks and other unwanted background noise. Strip Silence performs transient detection and then slices the audio into individual regions according to whatever adjustments you make to the various parameters in the window.

- Select an audio region in the Arrange window.
- Choose Strip Silence from the Audio menu (Audio > Strip Silence).
- Alternately, from the independent Audio Bin window (Window > Audio Bin), select Options > Strip Silence.
- Before processing, adjust the threshold, the minimum time to accept as silence, the pre-attack time and post-release time.
- A series of individual regions will be created out of the original region creating empty space between them, their size and number depending on your settings.

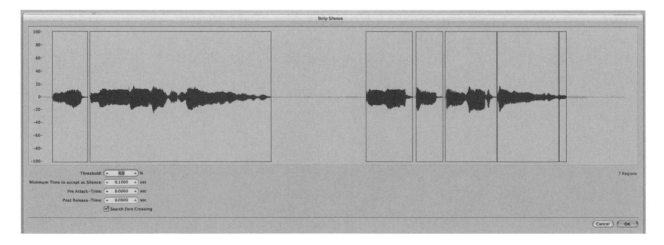

Figure 6.14: Strip Silence in the Audio menu

PART III: MIXING IN LOGIC

Chapter 7

Everything About the Mixer

Not only is recording in Logic easy when you know how, it has a number of advantages for the professional engineer, especially for large projects. To name a few examples, there are 255 possible channel strips in Logic, which is quite impressive compared with the limited voice count in other DAWs. Also, the Single mode introduced below is a unique tool for working on the sound of an instrument or voice that has complex routing to multiple auxiliary tracks.

The Logic Mixer has come into its own as being both professional and technically sound. In recent years it has incorporated features that are greatly appreciated by longtime Logic users and increasingly by professional engineers working in other studio environments.

First, a Tour of the Mix Window

The Mixer is accessed from the main Arrange window from the tab at the bottom, appropriately labeled Mixer. The tab is a toggle to bring the Mixer into and out of view.

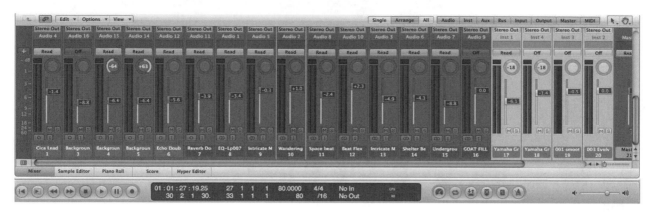

Figure 7.1: Accessing the Mixer

Whichever track is highlighted in the Arrange window will be selected in the Mixer, indicated with a lime-green rectangular halo around the channel strip.

Figure 7.2: Selected track in Mixer

Track input and output assignments can be modified on the channel strip beneath the sends and inserts, where it is labeled "I/O" for Input and Output assignment (Mixer > Options > I/O Labels).

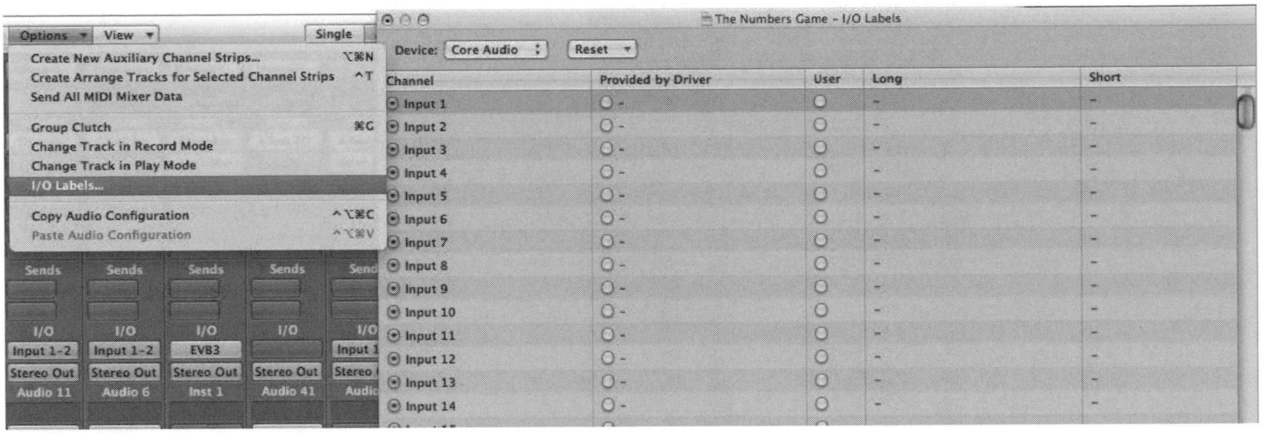

Figure 7.3: I/O Label assignments

The slider in the lower right of the Mixer, directly above the Transport bar, lets you adjust the width of the channel strips in your Mixer.

Figure 7.4: Adjusting width of channel strips

Channel Strip Settings for Plug-In Chains

Channel strip settings are an example of a Logic mixing feature that speeds up the workflow for every Logic user who discovers them. While they are visible in the main Arrange window and are a core part of the Arrange window workflow, they are also an essential building block of the work done in the Logic Mixer. Many Pro Tools engineers have their eye on this innovative system for saving and reloading an entire plug-in chain.

Channel strip settings are a configuration of plug-ins that combine, for example, an EQ and Compressor setting that work well together for a specific purpose. At the top of each channel strip is the pane for the channel strip setting with a pull-down menu when you click on it to load, save, and copy channel strip settings as well as a host of other options.

Figure 7.5: The channel strip setting menu

There are tons of fantastic factory channel strip settings that contain a combination of plug-in presets for specific mixing purposes, whether to problem-solve or to create a particular sound like a Clean or Warm Acoustic Guitar. They are grouped into categories by instrument (for example, Drums & Percussion, Electric Guitar) or voice.

There are also highly creative channel strip settings in the folders labeled Spaces, Warped, and Surround. The channel strip settings are available not only for audio tracks and software instrument tracks but also for the main output track—in effect, mastering and analysis settings. I have seen the Logic sessions of more than a few "hit" songs that have used Logic channel strip settings straight from the factory.

It really gets powerful when you start modifying the factory channel strip settings or creating your own from scratch for specific purposes, such as for your guitarist or your singer. These combinations of EQs, Compressors, Reverbs, and many more of Logic's 80-plus effects plug-ins are great starting points when the artist first gets on the microphone, so that he or she immediately sounds good.

After you tweak a plug-in chain for a particular situation or song, I recommend that you save it as a channel strip setting so that it shows up in your Library for you to use the next time your guitarist or singer is in that same mood, working on another ballad or up-tempo dance track. Then, only subtle adjustments need to be made for the specific situation.

Producer-musician Greg Kurstin has an extensive library of custom channel strip settings he has created for audio and software instrument tracks. His philosophy for building these settings is rather inspiring in its simplicity—and the success with hit records he continues to record and mix himself in his own studio for the likes of Lily Allen, Foster the People, K$sha, and many more.

It's a lot of trial and error. I never studied engineering. I'd listen to records I like and try to analyze what makes them sound the way they do. I'd listen to my track and compare it to something I really like that was mixed. I would read magazines or talk to engineer friends and ask them questions. Most of the time I was experimenting with plug-ins to fully understand what they do. One example is the Channel EQ. I'd grab it with the mouse almost like I'm molding the shape of it. Find frequencies that sound good boosted, or the opposite if there's something you want to remove.

The same with compression, just by moving the mouse around and hearing what something does. At first I didn't know about the attack and release scientifically. Just that this is what happens when I move the release this way. Then side chaining came after. It's just experimenting and listening to what it sounds like when I move the mouse a certain way.

I would just look at a plug-in instead of reading a manual of how it's supposed to work. I'd put up a sound and start pressing a button, moving a dial. I didn't really know conceptually what things are supposed to do necessarily.

Turn a knob, press a button, and use my ears to see what it does.

Kick drums and low end were always such a mystery to me.

Getting better speakers definitely helped. I was always afraid of the bass. I didn't know how big I could make it. I had to learn how to tighten it up and take out certain frequencies.

Even the kick drum and bass relationship is a whole thing. I'm constantly trying to solve that problem, whether it's with side chaining, EQ'ing.

I just use my ears. That's the bottom line. That sounds good, so I know it's right.

I live off of the channel strip settings. They are so important for working fast! I might have a synth and I want to make it more interesting with delays and modulation and filters, and I'll make big channel strip settings and save them and then remember that sound for another track. Especially on the soft synths but also the audio channels, sometimes for vocals, guitars, weird trippy guitar sounds with filters and delays. My library is a big mess, but I don't want to clean it up because I know where everything is. —*Greg Kurstin*

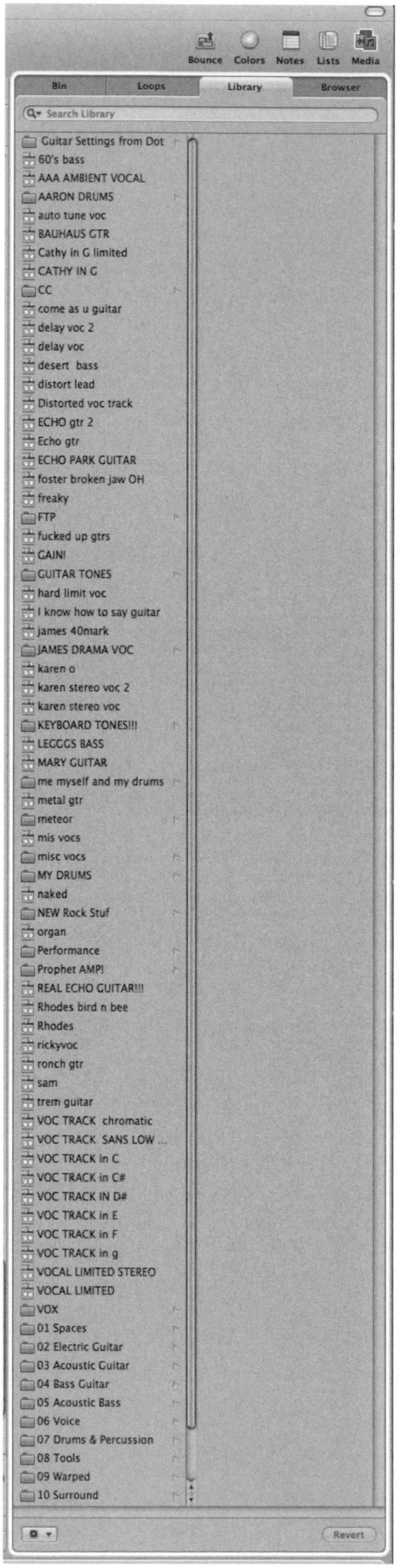

Figure 7.6: Greg Kurstin's library of settings

Power Tip: Using Software Instrument Settings on Audio Tracks (and vice versa)

You may find yourself working on the plug-in chain for a bass line recorded by a live bass player and then remember a perfect plug-in chain you created for a bass preset in the ES1 software instrument. The channel strip settings for software instruments and audio tracks are technically saved to separate folders (for example, Track, Master, or Instrument). You can see this organization when you look from the Finder and in the Library.

When you select an audio track, by default you see only the channel strip settings that were created for audio tracks, and vice versa if you select a software instrument track. Logic has a great solution for this fairly common situation. Option-click on the channel strip setting pane on top of a channel strip to access channel strip settings from a different type of track object, such as a software instrument channel strip setting, even though you're working on an audio track.

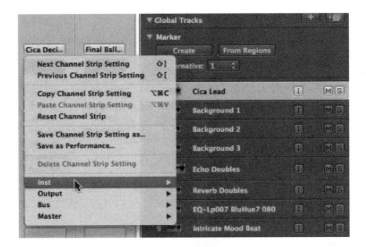

Figure 7.7: Option-click to access channel strip setting types

Creating Your Own Channel Strip Settings and Folders

You can create your own channel strip settings that will be available in the Library to the right of the Arrange window. To create your own channel strip setting, click-and-hold on the pane labeled Setting at the top of the channel strip setting. A menu appears with the Save Channel Strip Setting option. You can also scroll through the Library of existing channel strip settings from this pull-down menu on top of the channel strip. However, I recommend developing the habit of shopping for channel strip settings in the Library on the right side of the Arrange window. This is much more efficient for viewing all the subfolders at once. For one, you don't have to use your mouse to hold the view open as you do when clicking from the channel strip setting pane on the left. The folders in the Library remain open after you select one.

Figure 7.8: The channel strip setting menu

In addition to the many synth channel strip settings I've created for thick layered strings, twisted yet luxurious pads, deep basses, go-to favorite pianos and electric pianos, I always save the channel strip settings created by engineers visiting my studio for my singer and other live instrumentalists by the song name to easily access them when working on a song with a similar character. Third-party plug-ins can be stored in the chain of a channel strip setting as well.

You will probably want to create folders for your custom channel strip settings. When you select to save a channel strip setting from the channel strip setting pane, there is an option in the lower left to create a new folder. These custom folders will then be added to the Library in the Media section of the Arrange window on top of the factory channel strip settings, which are labeled "01 Logic Instruments, 02 Acoustic Pianos, 03 Bass, 04 Drums & Percussion," and so on.

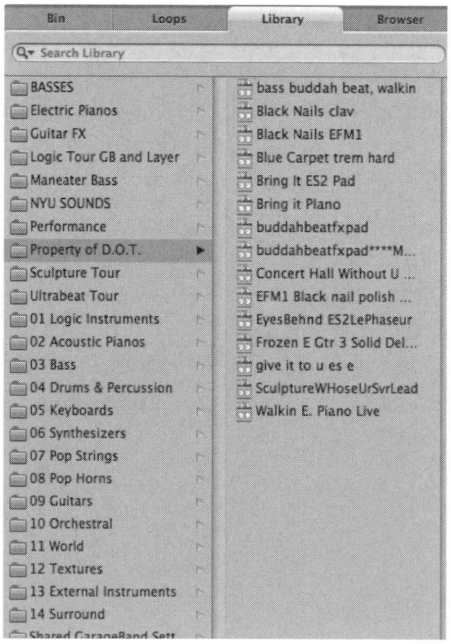

Figure 7.9: Custom channel strip settings in the Library

Mixer Views: Single View Versus Arrange View

The Mixer View buttons in the Mixer are a great system that will speed up your workflow enormously. These buttons are located in the upper right of the screen and are labeled Single, Arrange, and All. Whichever button is selected determines which group of tracks is in view.

Figure 7.10: Mixer Views

Arrange View is the most straightforward, displaying all the tracks in the Arrange window of the current project. Single mode is brilliant and unique to the Logic Mixer; it provides you with a view of the entire signal flow of a selected track, whether an audio track or a software instrument.

The main channel strip will be visible, as well as any auxiliary tracks and the main output, so you can isolate and focus on the complete sound of an instrument or voice and its signal path. This eliminates the laborious process of scrolling in your mixer past all 32, 64, or more audio tracks to the auxiliary tracks, where a vocal is bussed, for example.

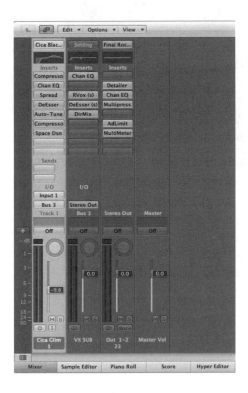

Figure 7.11: Single View in the Mixer

Between the two features of Single View and dynamic channel strip creation in the Arrange window (dual channel strips) that were introduced in chapter 1, you can easily follow the workflow practices of any professional engineer as far as bussing plug-ins to auxiliary tracks.

The secondary (and in some cases more significant) benefit is maximizing an efficient CPU load on your computer. For example, instead of creating the same plug-in chain on each of the four background vocals with an EQ, DeEsser, and Reverb using the same exact setting, you can create buses to one auxiliary track with all three plug-ins or three individual auxiliary tracks. Either way, you will have each effect loaded only one time—three instances, instead of 12 plug-ins weighing down your CPU. In the above illustration (Figure 7.11), the vocal track does have a number of plug-ins inserted directly on the channel that are unique to that vocal, but the output is routed to aux 3, where four effects are shared by other vocal tracks in the project.

The All View is simply the view of all possible tracks—audio tracks, software instrument tracks, auxiliary tracks, and so on. There are various instances in which this becomes useful—if, for example, you need to view and adjust levels on the Klopfgeist (Logic's peculiarly named metronome that translates from German as "ghost"), which defaults to audio track 128 and is generally not in the Arrange window view by default.

Figure 7.12: All View in Mixer

The other set of Mixer View buttons to be aware of are the buttons to the right that are labeled Audio, Inst, Aux, Bus, Input, Output, Master, and MIDI. These will isolate a type of track within each view you select—Single, Arrange, or All. This is very handy when you want to temporarily focus on your software instruments or aux tracks, for example.

The View buttons are especially helpful when you are revisiting an older project you haven't looked at in a while, getting familiar with someone else's Logic project, or simply working quickly in your own session.

Rearranging and Bypassing FX with the Hand Tool

The Mixer has Tool menus independent of the one in the Arrange window, as do all the Editor windows. The Hand tool is a great choice for the secondary tool when you are working in the Mixer.

Holding down the Command/Apple key accesses the Hand tool, and you can easily rearrange plug-ins on a track or between tracks. Simply highlight and drag up or down in the plug-in chain with the Hand tool. Additionally hold down the Option key while selecting the Hand tool when you want to copy a plug-in to another track.

Figure 7.13: Hand tool to rearrange plug-ins

To bypass a plug-in, Option-click and the plug-in will remain on the channel strip but appear grayed-out as opposed to blue, which indicates that the plug-in is active. You may want to bypass a plug-in for A/B'ing purposes, or it may be a creative decision to automate the bypass during a particular passage.

Figure 7.14: Option-click to bypass plug-in

Adding Mixer Tracks to the Arrange Window

To add a channel strip to the Arrange window, control-click anywhere on the channel strip and a contextual menu opens with the item Create/Select Arrange Track on top.

Figure 7.15: Create/Select Arrange
window track

Here's an example of when you might use this feature: In the Mixer, there is a Stereo Output channel strip labeled Output 1–2, as well as a Master channel strip. The Master controls the gain for all outputs if you are using multiple outputs for any external summing or mixing with a console. The Master channel strip by default does not appear in the Arrange window, but you may want to have it there to view its automation.

Figure 7.16: Master
versus Stereo Out
channel strip

Control-click on the Mixer channel strip to access the contextual menu to select or deselect the features to have in view on the channel strip, such as Sends, Inserts, Track Name, or EQ Thumbnail. Many objects in the Logic workspace have additional features accessed from a pull-down menu by Control-clicking. Take a quick look now at the options available on the channel strip.

Power Tip: Make Note!

When you Control-click on a Mixer channel strip, you'll notice Notes at the bottom of the list. This feature allows you to make quick notes about the settings you are adjusting to the channel.

Coloring Track Names

The track names at the bottom of each channel strip can be color-coded, just like your markers and regions in the Arrange window. It takes only a few extra seconds to do this, and you'll thank yourself. Practically speaking, your eye can quickly adjust to the visual grouping, and it becomes a subtle workflow enhancement in that you are able to find a particular instrument more quickly. For example, all your vocals can have a background color of red, all your drums can be blue, and so on.

To change the color, select Colors from the local View menu at the bottom of the list and then swipe across the track names at the bottom of the channel strips. Or, you can use the default key command of Option + C.

Figure 7.17: Coloring your Mixer track names

Temporary Track Grouping

Creating groups in Logic will be covered in the next section of this chapter. While you're here in the Mixer, there is a great way to temporarily group tracks for adjusting gain, adding a send, and so on. Drag over adjacent tracks and they will become highlighted and placed in a temporary group. To add nonadjacent tracks, hold down the Shift key as you drag over the tracks. Click off to deselect the temporary group.

Mono Outputs

Click on the small circle at the bottom of the channel strip, directly above its name, to toggle between mono and stereo. Mono is indicated by a single circle, and stereo by two interlocking circles.

Next, click-and-hold on the output assignment panel in the I/O area above, and select Output > Mono at the bottom of the menu and then make your assignment of the specific output. This is helpful when you're mixing out to a console or other summing hardware rather than mixing in the box.

Figure 7.18: Temporary track grouping in the Mixer

Figure 7.19: Mono outputs

Creating Track Groups

You can create track groups in the Arrange window as well as the Mixer, and track groups are just as relevant for editing as for mixing. Once you get the hang of how quickly you can create and bypass groups, you'll be using them in many engineering situations.

Creating a Group

To create a group, click on the group slot of a channel strip and then choose to open group settings. Within the settings, you can individually select which parameters will be controlled as a group—Volume, Mute, Pan, Solo, Editing, and so on. Once a track is assigned to a group, the group number will be visible on the group slot.

Figure 7.20: Group slot
on a channel strip

Below are a few helpful group assignment shortcuts:
- To assign a track to multiple groups, press Shift while choosing a group.
- To assign a track to the most recent group settings, Option-click on the Group slot.
- In the Settings window, you may want to enable the checkbox next to Phase-Locked Audio for any heavy lifting of editing grouped tracks.

Disabling a Group: Group Clutch

Group Clutch is the term in Logic used for disabling track groups when you want to make adjustments to a track individually. To temporarily disable all groups, choose Options > Group Clutch or the key command that defaults to Option + G. When the groups are disabled, the group slots change color from yellow to light gray. Note: There is no option in Logic to disable a single group, only all groups at once.

To automate tracks in a group, select any member of the group to make a mix or editing adjustment. Automation will be covered in the next chapter.

Surround in Logic

Logic has a thorough surround capability that is available free as built-in functionality. I've met more than a few Pro Tools engineers who use surround in Logic for this reason alone. The surround panner can be accessed on the Arrange channel strip or in the Mixer on a channel strip for positional mixing in the surround field.

The Surround Preferences are accessed from the I/O Assignments tab in the Audio Preferences (Preferences > Audio > I/O Assignments > Surround). Here you assign which outputs of your interface are connected to which speaker, and which inputs of your interface will be used.

The Format setting in the New Tracks window is also where you set up your surround input and output. If you select Surround, both the input and output can be assigned accordingly.

The surround panner will automatically be introduced on the channel strip to make surround assignments. Double-click to open as a separate window. Special note: You need to assign channel strips to surround output in order to view the surround plug-ins.

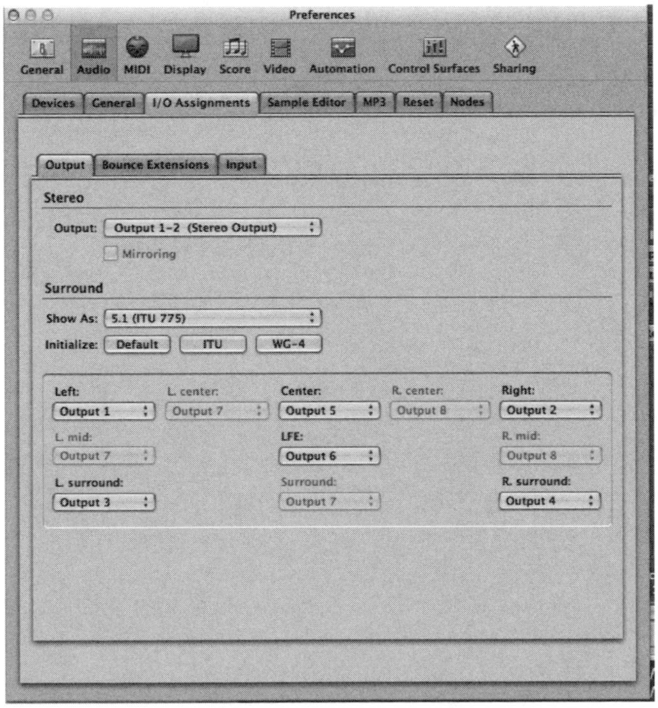

Figure 7.21: Surround I/O assignment in audio preferences

Logic supports the following surround formats: LCRS Surround, 5.1 Surround, 6.1 Surround, 7.1 Surround, and 7.1 SDDS-Sony DDS Sound Surround. By default, the surround format is set to 5.1 in a new project.

Logic offers a number of surround effect plug-ins and surround versions of the Sculpture and ES2 software instruments. These will be visible on any insert slot when the channel strip output is set to Surround. Multichannel plug-ins have an advanced plug-in header.

Bouncing in surround will create multiple audio files, each identified by a unique extension. File name extensions are determined in the Bounce Extensions preference (Preferences > Audio > I/O Assignments > Output).

More Power Tips and Tricks for Mixing in Logic

This next section offers a few simple tricks every professional working in Logic should have under their fingertips. Some techniques are for daily use, such as bypassing plug-ins, creating a shortcut to your aux channels, or reordering plug-ins on a channel, while others are for more specialized troubleshooting situations like adjusting the linear meter scale, Solo Safe mode, or the Pan Law assignment.

Bypass Plug-Ins

Option-click on the blue pane of a plug-in inserted on a channel strip to bypass it. Option-click again to restore it to being active on the channel.

Linear Meter Scale

There are two ways to view the level on a channel strip. The Level Meters Scale pop-up menu (Preferences > Display > Mixer > Level Meters) switches the level meters between a Sectional dB-linear scale and an Exponential scale. Exponential provides a higher display resolution in the upper range of the meter. Sectional dB-linear provides the best possible display resolution across the entire level range.

Solo Safe

When a channel strip is in Solo Safe mode, it remains audible even when other channel strips are soloed. Solo Safe is indicated by a diagonal red line through the Solo button on a channel strip. Control-click on the Solo button to toggle the Solo Safe status.

Figure 7.22: Solo Safe mode

When Solo Safe Mode Misbehaves

There are times when you may find that a particular audio channel strip in a project reverts to Solo Safe mode when you load the project, even after you manually disable Solo Safe. This is because a Logic project contains an audio channel strip used for prelistening to audio in the Sample Edit window, Audio Bin, and Loop Browser. When you create a Logic project from one of the factory templates, this channel strip is assigned to Audio 256. This channel strip stays in Solo Safe mode so that you can always preview audio. The image below shows the channel strip for a new, empty project.

If there is no audio channel strip in a project assigned to Audio 256, Logic will use the highest-numbered available audio channel for prelistening. When the project is loaded, that channel strip will be put into Solo Safe mode. You may find that this happens in older projects or in those cases where you have deleted the Audio 256 channel strip in a project.

The Pan Law

The Pan Law value determines the amount of volume reduction on signals panned to the center position. Signals in Logic panned center may sound louder than those panned hard right or left. The setting in Logic differs from the one in Pro Tools, and this can throw off engineers who have been working in the Pro Tools environment. The –3 dB compensated value that is the default in Logic makes sense for users who are "mixing in the box." This setting leaves the output up the middle flat and cuts the signal –3 db at far left and right. This ensures that if you send signal to a channel with the panner at its straight-up-the-middle default position, the output is the same as what is coming in.

Pro Tools engineers working with an external console expect a different default that cuts the signal in the middle, but leaves it intact when panned left or right. That really only makes sense if you are sending discrete signals to a console by panning them alternatively left or right, as they would do. The Pan Law is a setting, and not a preference in Logic, which means it is project specific. To adjust, select Settings > Audio.

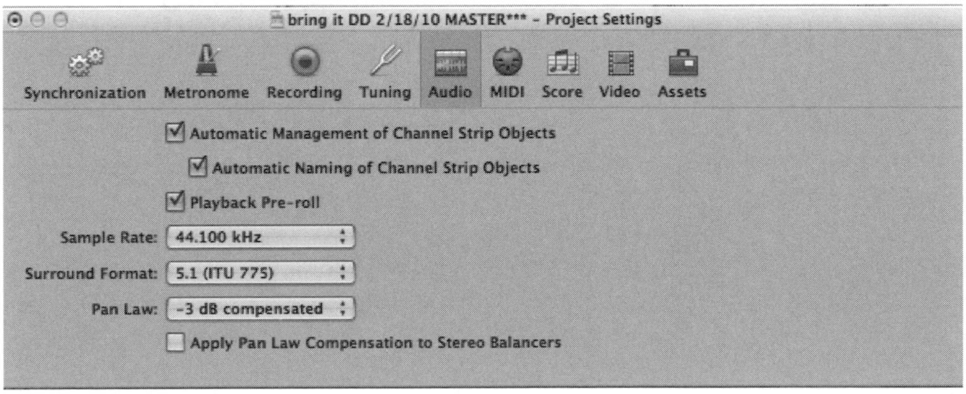

Figure 7.23: Default Pan Law of –3dB

A Shortcut to Your Aux Channels

Double-click on a mixer assignment (such as a bus, an aux, an output, and so on), and Logic will take you right to that destination in the Mixer. This eliminates the need to scroll through the Mixer, which can be especially time-consuming with larger sessions.

Reordering and Rearranging Plug-Ins

Use the Hand tool to move plug-ins up and down on a channel strip or to another channel strip.

Bigger Is Better:
Adjusting Waveform Size and Plug-In Size

The slider with a graphic display of a waveform in the bottom right of the Arrange window is used to adjust the waveform scale within a region.

To increase the size of a plug-in, drag on the lower-right-hand corner and you can extend the size of the plug-in to be as large as your monitor.

Chapter 8

AUTOMATION IN LOGIC
(HAS ITS ADVANTAGES)

Automation in Logic can be performed on every parameter of every plug-in as well as on the basics of volume, pan, and aux send controls. This means that all movements of faders, knobs, and switches can be recorded, edited, and played back in your project. The automation is sample-accurate, so it's extremely precise. Logic's automation has a few core advantages over other DAWs that make it convenient and visually pleasing to many professional Logic users, and these advantages will be covered in this chapter.

The Basics of Automation in Logic

Automation data in Logic is created on the automation tracks. Audio waveforms or MIDI notes are visible at a reduced contrast beneath the automation data. The automation data is seen as colored lines and dots, which are the nodes of automation. Numerical values are displayed at each node in decibels.

Viewing Automation

There are a few different ways to enable the view of automation. Click on the Automation button in the Arrange toolbar, select View > Track Automation in the Arrange window, or choose the key command Hide/Show Track Automation, which defaults to the A key. The Automation Parameter menu is displayed in the track header, and the gray automation area appears on all tracks. You can now choose the parameter to automate, which will default to Volume with the mode set to "Read."

Figure 8.1: Automation view

The Automation Parameter Menu

Here you can now experience one of the conveniences of Logic's automation. In the Automation Parameter menu on the track header, you will see every parameter of every plug-in available for automating as well as Volume and Pan for each track.

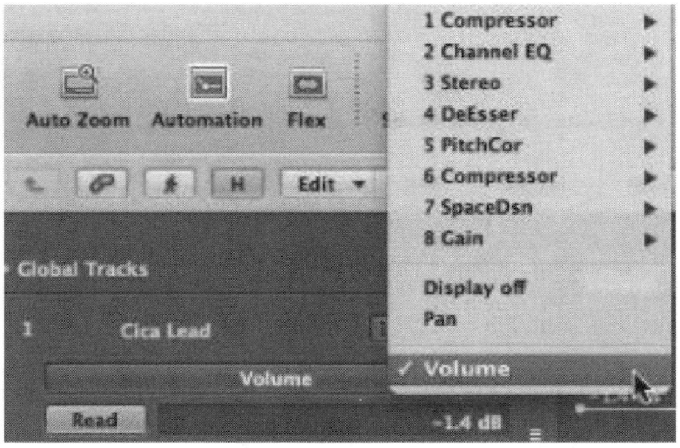

Figure 8.2: Automation Parameter menu on track header

Automation Lanes

Another great convenience is that you can view all the automation lanes on a track simultaneously. Click on the disclosure triangle to the lower left of the track name in the track list. Option-click to open up all the automation subtracks at once. This is a toggle—Option-click again to collapse the view of automation subtracks.

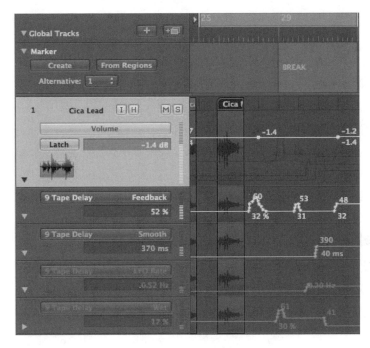

Figure 8.3: View of all automation lanes on a track

Automation Modes for Creating Automation Data

The automation mode determines whether automation is being written, read, or turned off, and if it is being written, how. This is selected in the track header's Automation Mode menu that defaults to "Read," or you can select it directly on a channel strip. Option-click to select the same automation mode for all channel strips and Shift-click on a group of channel strips to assign an automation mode to those selected tracks. This can all be assigned by key command. In the Key Commands window, type "Automation" in the search field in the upper right to locate the relevant key commands. See the section "Key Commands: The Secret to Learning Logic (condensed)" in chapter 10 for a summary of the steps for making your own key command assignments.

You can record track automation data once an automation mode is selected, whether Logic is in Record or Playback mode. The modes of automation in Logic will be familiar to the Pro Tools engineer because they are essentially the same: Off, Read, Touch, Latch, and Write—with Touch and Latch being the most popular modes for creating automation data.

With Touch mode, a parameter returns to its previous setting when you release the fader, knob, or whatever else you're using to create the data. With Latch mode, the automation parameter stays "latched" wherever you move it to, the current value replacing any existing automation data ahead on the track. With Write mode, existing track automation data is erased as the playhead passes it. This destructive Write mode of automation is likely one you will rarely use.

The best way to erase automation data is by choosing Track > Track Automation > Delete All Automation on Selected Track (or Delete All Automation).

Figure 8.4: The four automation modes

Writing and Editing Track Automation Data

After selecting your automation mode, you are ready to create automation data by moving a fader or control on a selected layer of automation.

With the Pointer or Pencil tool, create nodes of automation by clicking on or just outside an automation line. If the tracks are grouped, the node will be created on all tracks in the group if the checkboxes were selected in the group settings for volume, pan, sends, and so on.

Automation Select Tool

You can zoom in and edit the breakpoints on an individual track with exacting detail, and then draw in new automation manually just by clicking with your Pointer or Pencil tool. Or, switch to the Automation Select tool to drag select nodes of automation or between two automation nodes.

Below are a few techniques for working with the Automation Select tool:

- Drag on a selected area to move all the selected nodes.
- Shift-click on the selection while using the Automation Select tool is a toggle to deselect a node.
- Clicking outside a line or node, within the selected area, changes all values proportionately by a percentage value.
- Here's a good one: Option + double-click when no nodes are selected. This will select all automation data, which you can move forward or backward, up or down, independent of the audio or MIDI region.

You definitely want to experiment with the Automation Select tool to develop speed and control with it. You may find that you prefer using the Pointer or Pencil tool, the key commands, or the Track Automation menu items covered below.

Figure 8.5: Automation Select tool

The Track Automation Menu

Take a few minutes to explore the Automation menu options in the local Track menu in the Arrange window. Automation is the first item on the list, with a number of other handy automation selection techniques.

For example, to create one node at each region border, do one of the following:

1. Select the region, then choose Track > Track Automation > Create Nodes at Region Borders.
2. Select the Automation Select tool, then Option-click the region header area.

To create two automation nodes at each region border, which will allow you to quickly create rides in the automation data, do one of the following:

1. Select the region, then choose Track > Track Automation > Create Two Nodes at Region Borders.
2. Select the Automation Select tool, then Control + Option + Shift-click on the region header area.

In the menu are also a number of options for deleting automation data, whether on an entire lane or layer of automation, on one track, or on all tracks. These operations can also be completed with the respective key command. If you find yourself doing these operations often, you're best off assigning key commands.

Figure 8.6: Automation submenu in local track menu

Snap Automation

Snap Automation in the Snap and Drag modes (introduced in the section "Editing at Maximum Speed" in chapter 3) snaps automation to the resolution set in the transport, depending on the zoom level. The resolution is defined the same way as for other editing snaps. This allows you to efficiently "snap" automation to the timeline. If you like to do crazy bends, maybe play in some cutoff wobbles and tweaks over a piece of existing MIDI, and maybe experiment with sliders and knobs on an external controller, you will find Snap Automation quite helpful. Maybe you want to move the automation onto a later part of the grid. Snap automation will allow you to avoid the guesswork involved in selecting exactly one bar, and sliding it over by exactly one bar.

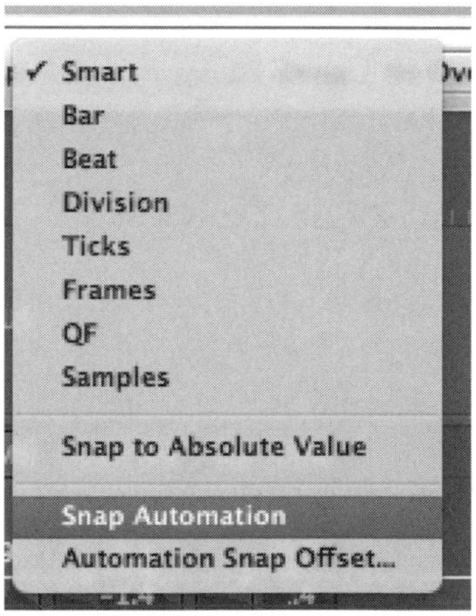

Figure 8.7: Snap Automation

Moving and Editing Automation

Here are a number of techniques that you may find helpful when working with automation in Logic:

- To copy automation within a track, select the nodes or lines you want to copy, and then Option-drag them to the new location.
- To copy automation to another track, hold down the Shift key while dragging a selection, or select copy and paste.
- Choose Edit > Copy, and then select the track you want to copy automation data to and choose Edit > Paste (the default key commands are Command + C and Command + V).
- To move automation data, select the nodes or lines and drag. Hold the Control key while dragging for fine adjustment of the automation node or line value.
- A great trick introduced in the section "The Essential Marquee Tool," in chapter 3, is to Marquee-select across any area of automation, then when you click back in with the Pointer tool, four nodes are created. This allows you to easily draw in volume rides, or other automation parameter rides.
- To copy the automation data of one parameter to another, Command-click on and then select the parameter in the Automation Parameter menu. A dialog box will ask if you want to convert or copy the automation data from the source parameter. Then Command-click into the same menu to choose the destination parameter. Each layer of automation will be a different color, which is quite easy on the eye.

A major convenience with Logic automation is that you can view all lanes of automation simultaneously. Simply click on the disclosure triangle on the lower left of the track header to view the next lane beneath or Option-click to view all lanes of automation at once.

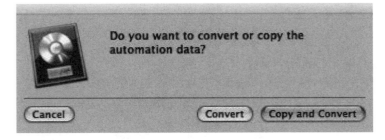

Figure 8.8: Automation Parameter menu dialog box to copy data

Automation Preferences

You can move regions with or independent from track automation data depending on your assignment in the Automation Preferences (Logic Pro > Preferences > Automation > Move Automation with Region). You'll have the option to include the automation data Never, Always, or to view a dialog box each time, allowing you to manually decide whether to move the automation with the region.

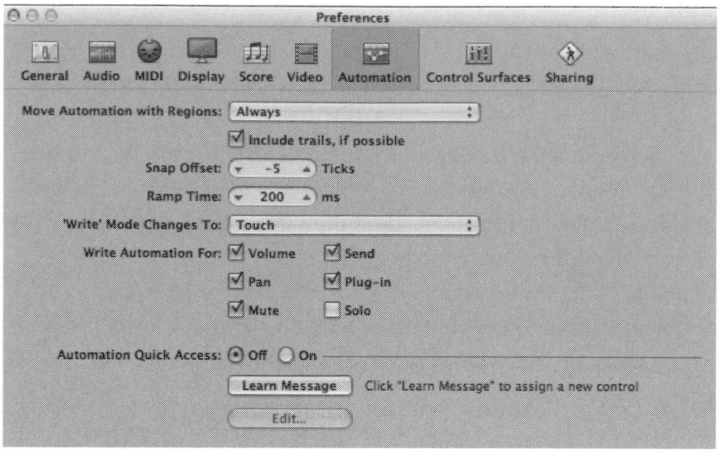

Figure 8.9: Automation Preferences

Trimming Automation by Lane

You can adjust the relative level of an entire lane of automation on a track in the track header by dragging up or down in the value slider while holding down the Command key.

Figure 8.10: Adjusting automation level on a lane

Track Automation Event List

There is one final concept to grasp when it comes to automation in Logic. There is an event list specifically for automation data that you may prefer using for edits at particular points in the timeline. This event list is a bit of a secret. You can open it only by using a key command! The default is Ctrl + Command + E. In this event list, automation events are displayed as MIDI controller data. They can be adjusted very precisely as far as their length and value.

bring it DD 2/18/10 MASTER***:Automation:Cica Lead – Event List

Edit ▾ | Functions ▾ | View ▾

Filter | Create | off (3840)

| Notes | Progr. Change | Pitch Bend | Controller |
| Chnl Pressure | Poly Pressure | Syst. Exclusive | Additional Info |

Position				Status	Ch	Num	Val	Length/Info
1	1	1	1	Fader	10	3	30	Feedback
1	1	1	1	Fader	10	9	4	Smooth
1	1	1	1	Fader	10	12	10	LFO Rate
1	1	1	1	Fader	10	20	30	Wet
1	1	1	1	Control	1	7	73	Volume
18	4	4	240	Control	1	7	73	Volume
19	1	1	1	Control	1	7	73	Volume
19	3	1	240	Control	1	7	73	Volume
19	3	2	1	Control	1	7	75	Volume
19	4	3	237.	Control	1	7	75	Volume
19	4	3	238.	Control	1	7	73	Volume
21	2	4	240	Control	1	7	73	Volume
21	3	1	1	Control	1	7	76	Volume
22	2	2	185	Control	1	7	76	Volume
22	2	2	186	Control	1	7	73	Volume
23	3	4	240	Control	1	7	73	Volume
23	4	1	1	Control	1	7	76	Volume
24	2	2	112.	Control	1	7	76	Volume
24	2	2	113.	Control	1	7	73	Volume
27	2	4	49.	Fader	10	3	30	Feedback
27	2	4	130.	Fader	10	3	31	Feedback
27	2	4	160.	Fader	10	3	32	Feedback
27	2	4	182.	Fader	10	3	37	Feedback
27	2	4	222.	Fader	10	3	41	Feedback
27	3	1	17.	Fader	10	3	49	Feedback
27	3	1	42.	Fader	10	3	53	Feedback
27	3	1	80.	Fader	10	3	57	Feedback
27	3	1	106.	Fader	10	3	59	Feedback
27	3	1	169.	Fader	10	3	60	Feedback
27	3	2	30.	Fader	10	3	61	Feedback
27	3	3	130.	Fader	10	3	61	Feedback
27	3	3	132.	Fader	10	3	62	Feedback
27	3	3	165.	Fader	10	3	63	Feedback

Cica Lead

Figure 8.11: Track Automation Event List

Chapter 9

MUST-HAVE LOGIC PLUG-INS FOR MIXING

The effects plug-ins included with Logic Pro decidedly sound fantastic and are easy to use. Best of all is their seamless integration in Logic. They work efficiently in Logic as far as your CPU is concerned, and will be authorized on all computers where you have Logic installed. It is a real challenge to pick only a few Logic plug-ins to showcase when so many of them are extraordinary, professional tools. Then there are the many brilliant third-party plug-ins you can get to complement this Logic suite—to name any here without naming all of them would be a grave injustice, but don't hold back from exploring these alternate universes of sound in Logic.

Without covering all 80 Logic effects plug-ins, a few favorites are featured in this chapter to provide you with a taste of the caliber of effects that come with Logic. I've enlisted two Logic-based professional engineers, Chris "Stone" Garrett and Rick Sheppard—both of whom work in Logic by choice—to provide insights into a few favorite Logic plug-ins and their distinguishing features. A third special guest is the multitalented Greg Kurstin, who fits the description introduced in the preface of a Logic musician-turned-engineer. He remains a successful songwriter and producer for the likes of Lily Allen, Foster the People, the Shins, and Ke$ha but is able to professionally record and mix in his own studio himself these projects that he produces.

Channel EQ: Logic's Multiband EQ

Logic has a fantastic suite of seven equalizer (or EQ) plug-ins to shape your sound by providing you with control over the level of specific frequency bands. Equalization is obviously one of the most fundamental processing techniques for audio. EQs are essentially filters that allow certain frequencies to pass through unchanged while boosting or cutting the level of other frequencies. Parametric and multiband EQs like the Channel EQ allow for precise control.

The Basics of the Channel EQ

The Channel EQ is a multiband EQ with eight frequency bands and a series of great filters. Multiband EQs allow you to independently set the frequency, bandwidth, and Q factor of each frequency band, offering extremely precise control on either an individual sound or your entire mix. The Analyzer on the left and graphic controls make it easy to manipulate the sound in real time. The central area of the window is the graphic display for shaping each EQ band. You can just drag horizontally or vertically to shape each of the frequency bands, which are conveniently indicated by a different color. The buttons on top are toggles to turn the eight different filters on and off.

The Channel EQ is one of the first plug-ins that comes to mind for "Stone" Garrett, the very talented engineer for Thievery Corporation and their ESL Music label, who recorded and mixed their song "Numbers Game," which was included with the original release of Logic 9 (Arrange window > Help > Exploring Logic Pro Demo Project).

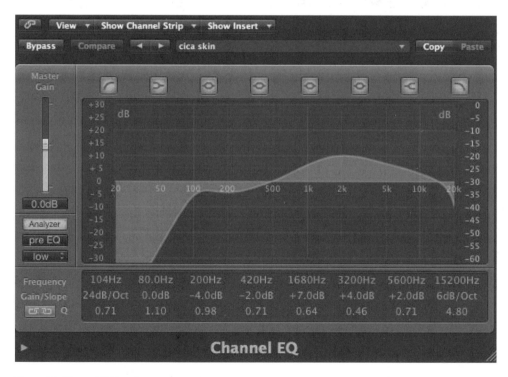

Figure 9.1: Channel EQ interface

An Example: Setting the Channel on a Male Vocal

The Logic Channel EQ is a standby for me. I do use the Universal Audio's UAD Cambridge and Pultec EQs for specific situations when I want something to sound a certain way. But otherwise, I always put the Logic Channel EQ on top of each channel strip, first in the signal path. It's just a personal preference to EQ first, then dynamics. Depending on the situation, maybe there will be a noise eliminator next, then reverb and delay—more "sound designy" stuff.

The configurability of the Logic EQ is what I like the most about it. The Analyzer is a standout feature. The fact that you can go pre or post on the Analyzer is extremely helpful for me.

I'm almost always a subtractive EQ type of guy—it sounds better to take things away than adding. That's not to say I wont push in some situations. On the Chuck Brown vocal in "Numbers Game," if you pull up that channel strip, you can see that I made dramatic cuts at the low end of 54 Hz. You're not going to want anything there! There's a dip of around 300 Hz and a tiny push right around 1,500 Hz. I'm trying to bring out a little of the high mid lows and hold back the low mid frequencies.

The parameters I use frequently are the high and low cut. I like the wide degree of choices of slopes. You can make a sharp cut or an easy slope.

First thing I do is turn on the Analyzer and look for peaks. I'll usually go to a higher resolution under the Analyzer, look, listen, and figure out where I want to make some cuts. The way to make your mix sound good is to get rid of frequencies that poke through the mix and hurt your ear. You want to calm everything down. I've done that here with the two small cuts.

The Channel EQ also has very good filters. I've used this EQ for effects where you automate a sweep on a beat or something you've worked up as part of the song where you want a low cut that sweeps. Because it's native to Logic, it's especially easy to automate—every single feature of the EQ is right there to automate.

For example, I'll take all of the rhythm section without the bass guitar, bounce it to a single file, and filter that as a very gradual sweep over an 8- or a 16-bar period to get that classic synthesizer filter. I might use the EQ's High Pass and Low Pass for that, too. Having the parametric control along with the filter sweep emulating what you would do with an analog filter, but having precise control over the automation, can make it a better tool than even a hardware alternative. —*Chris "Stone" Garrett*

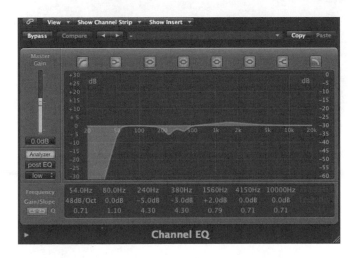

Figure 9.2: Chuck Brown vocals in "Numbers Game" by Thievery Corporation

Power Tip: Channel EQ Versus Linear Phase EQ

The Channel EQ and Linear Phase EQ in Logic have identical parameters, you can exchange settings between the two. The only distinction with the Linear Phase EQ is that it uses a fixed amount of CPU resources regardless of the number of active bands and maintains phase coherency that can introduce greater latency, and so is not recommended when you are playing software instruments but is more so recommended for mastering situations.

Multimeter for Phase Issues and Other Modern Mix Problems

The Multimeter provides a collection of four gauge and analysis tools in one plug-in window (Inserts > Helper > Multimeter) and is a great tool for your main output or, as "Stone" Garrett recommends, for every channel of your mix. The Multimeter has an Analyzer to view the level for each 1/3-octave frequency band, a Goniometer for phase coherency, a Correlation Meter for mono phase compatibility, and an Integrated Level Meter to view the signal for the left and right channels independently.

You can view either the Analyzer or Goniometer results in the main display area, depending on which you select on the left side of the plug-in.

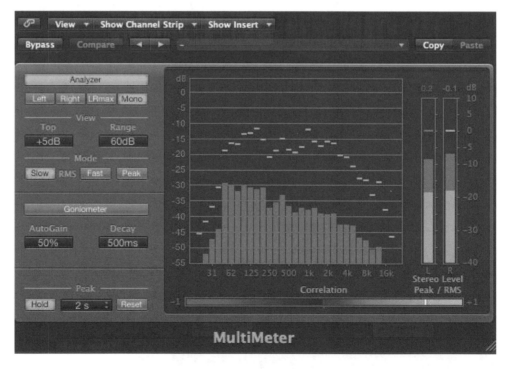

Figure 9.3: The Multimeter

Multimeter is another plug-in I use on almost every channel strip. I don't leave it on for the final mix but put it on as a tool all the way through until I start running out of computer juice, then I'll start taking off. There are two modes. One shows your stereo field, and the other is your spectral analyzer based on a set of octaves. Very simply, with the Analyzer I can choose between the sum or a separate left and right—the four tabs right under the Analyzer. The range is pretty self-explanatory of how many dBs you're seeing in your window, from 80 to 20 dB. I find myself using the Top feature under View that goes significantly over zero so you can see what's poking out to adjust what you're seeing. I'll adjust per channel to see if anything is lurking that needs getting rid of or other adjustment.

I flip through all the modes—slow, fast, peak, RMS—and have a close look at everything. Generally by this point if the Multimeter is on the main output channel, you don't want to see anything poking through. I'm sort of looking for a curve. I don't necessarily look for an even curve; I usually strive for something a little bottom heavy. I'll have a few dB between what's peaking and the rest. (The small orange squares are the peaks.) I'll check this on almost every channel strip then get rid of them, then just remove the plug-in.

Just to be clear, the Multimeter doesn't do anything to the sound—it's just for metering. I'll take a careful look at the Analyzer on the Channel EQ and the Multimeter. They are very different representations. The Multimeter is an octave meter, so it's a set of predetermined measuring (31, 62 ... the octaves in hertz and kilohertz of the frequencies, the numbered representation of the notes or frequencies). 440, the guitar tuning, would be in the octave band between 250 and 500. I usually keep the Peak at two seconds because I like a quick view of things. The Goniometer is great to check the Left/Right balance and have a look at any panning.

The Correlation Meter at the bottom is your phase meter, and this is very important. You want it on the blue side to the right. If you're in the red, you're out of phase. The way you fix it if you are out of phase is to go to the Logic Gain plug-in under Utility and hit Phase Invert.

You can have one thing out of phase that will do horrible things to your mix. Samples are notorious for being out of phase, because left and right is reversed. At some point during the sampling process, left and right gets swapped if the turntable isn't plugged in right, red to red, or a wire is crossed. The needle can even be out of phase, the stylus picking up a stereo image.

Some things are put on vinyl out of phase. It sounds like a very wide stereo mix if it's out of phase, just sounds weird—something sounds like it's coming from the corner of the room behind me, like a weird tickle. It may have a weird wide sound, or sound really bass heavy, or you might have a sample that has a slamming 808 drop, but when you sample it in it's wimpy. That's another good indicator that you have a phase problem.

Think about it in a 360-degree idea, that something is turned around backward. If you were out of phase by180 degrees, you would be turned around backward. It's one of those "ghosty" things. They make phase meters because it's hard to tell sometimes! —Chris "Stone" Garrett

Space Designer

The interface of the Space Designer convolution reverb is, quite simply, stunning. While a brilliant reverb to place your music in realistic re-creations of acoustic environments, Space Designer is much more than a reverb. It is aptly described as space modeling and design. Have a listen to the massive folders of factory presets and you'll have to agree.

The concept in brief of a convolution reverb is to introduce an impulse response (IR) reverb sample, which is a recording of a room's reverb characteristic. The idea is to take a sine wave sweep—an Impulse—and record it in a particular space, whether a church or a bathroom. Afterward, you remove the sine wave from the recording through a process called deconvolution. You are then left with a recording of the room space or, more specifically, a recording of all reflections in the room. This is the "response function," or IR (impulse response). The IR is an actual .aif file, a standard audio file. Savvy location recording engineers may even create impulse responses on site to have as backup afterward for any dialogue or other sound replacement.

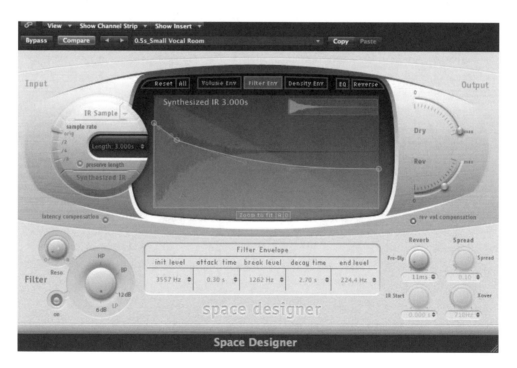

Figure 9.4: Space Designer's stunning interface

Longtime Logic-based engineer Rick Sheppard named it one of his must-have Logic plug-ins, and you'll learn why in this section.

I use Space Designer for my vocals and cymbals. It's a really good-sounding reverb and has a lot of nice plates and impulse responses with it. At the same time, it's really simple to tweak, it's super stable, and it's not a big memory hog.

I use the Reverse whenever I want to do cool vocal effects for remixes. In this project, I placed the Delay Designer on this first vocal bit, then end it with another audio bit going through Space Designer with Reverse to finish the vocal effect. The actual audio is one word "You"—cut and copied to another track with Space Designer

Reverse reverb time. You can adjust the length in the center window area with the IR knob. Make it completely wet with the reverb at max and the dry at minimum on the right.

The sample rate on the left is a quick way to adjust the length of the reverb time, dividing the sample rate. It's similar to changing the sample rate in Bit Crusher, but in this case it changes the length of the effect.

Such a simple easy layout! You select a tab and just draw. It makes it fun. —*Rick Sheppard (longtime engineer-programmer for producer Dallas Austin)*

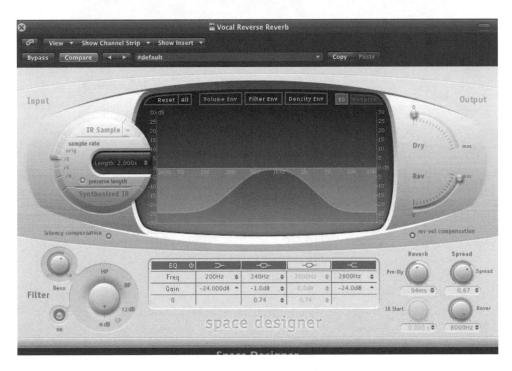

Figure 9.5: Rick Sheppard's Space Designer setting with reverse reverb

Compressor

Most musicians are familiar with the task of a compressor, which falls under the umbrella of dynamics processors and is one of the most essential tools of the engineer. The compressor reduces the difference in dynamic range between the loudest and quietest parts of a piece of music by automatically turning down the gain when the signal exceeds a predetermined level, and ensuring that softer sounds are not entirely lost in the mix.

The suite of dynamics processors that come with Logic include the Compressor, Expanders, Limiters, and Noise Gates. Below are some real-world examples from our Logic-based professional engineers about their everyday use of the Logic Compressor.

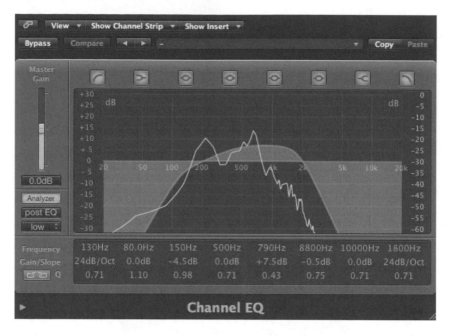

Figure 9.6: The Logic Compressor

Bread and Butter Compression with Compressor

The Logic Compressor is another reliable, standby plug-in for me. I use it very frequently. First of all, one of the neatest things is the circuit. I love that you can change the circuit type. It's very unique that you can just flip between them. I find myself going with the OPTO and FET a lot. We have a Peavey VCL-2 at the studio, which is an older compressor/limiter, and the sound the Logic Compressor gets is very close. OPTO uses a light sensor to adjust the attack of the compressor. Nothing is faster than the speed of light, so using light to sense the shape of the waveform is very effective.

With the Logic Compressor, I'll set the attack and release to Auto to automatically set the attack and release with a software algorithm and respond to any changing dynamics, set the circuit to OPTO, and achieve results surprisingly similar to this old-school, high-end Peavey compressor. It doesn't get the crunchy colorization, but the way the compressor reacts to what you put through it is very similar.

I use a very light-handed touch on compression unless I'm going for the effect of crushing the sound. When I want things to sound natural or enhance in the mix, I'll try and keep it to a minimum—never more than 6 dB on the compressor, and usually less than 3 dB. Not that I'm thinking about it while I'm setting the Compressor, but I'm just noticing it now. I'll use the FET one for bass and the OPTO one more for vocals.

Also, the limiter feature is very handy so you're not blowing up your channel. Try to keep it subtle. Nothing sounds good 20 dB deep into a limiter. It doesn't matter how great the limiter is. Obviously it has the on/off button. In this instance with Chuck's vocals, I have it on. You can see it activating when you play the track. I have the limiter threshold set pretty high. The Limiter has an on/off button. When you turn off the limiter, you can see we're 5 dB over on that channel. When you turn it on, we're just under 6 dB.

In a lot of cases, I'll try three different compressors on a channel to A/B which one sounds best. Sometimes I'll just flip through the presets and customize them. —*Chris "Stone" Garrett*

Figure 9.7: Compressor setting on Chuck Brown's vocals

Sidechain Effects for Dance Music

Using a sidechain inside a compressor is very popular and based on a simple concept. The level changes of an audio track are applied as a control source inside the compressor inserted on a second audio track. For example, an audio track containing a drum groove can be selected inside the sidechain of a compressor inserted onto a guitar track to dynamically change the compression and and rhythmic experience of the guitar part with the same pulse of the drum groove.

> I like sidechaining with a kick in the Logic Compressor to create a pulsing effect in the track. You can do this on the whole mix, on individual keyboard tracks, or on subgroups of instruments. It can be too much on the whole mix, so it's often better to pick a group of instruments. —*Rick Sheppard*

Here are Rick Sheppard's steps to achieving the sidechaining effect:
- Create a four-on-the-floor kick in a drum machine like Ultrabeat and loop it.
- Move it off the beat so it's on the "and" and not on the downbeat.
- Create a ducker setting in Compressor to pull down a part of the mix (see Figure 9.8).
- The definitive parameters for the ducker to achieve the pulsing effect is the Ratio cranked (30:1) and low Attack (10 ms or less), then use the Compressor Threshhold to adjust the desired amount. The Attack determines the speed of the pulse.
- Assign the output of the drum machine to an empty bus and assign the sidechain of the Compressor to that bus so that the kick is feeding the sidechain.

In this example, the drum machine sends to Bus 30 using the send, with no output on the track. Bus 30 goes to an aux automatically but with no output. Bring up the Compressor threshold three-fourths of the way. —*Rick Sheppard*

Figure 9.8: Rick Sheppard's Compressor sidechain

Delay Designer

Logic has an incredible suite of delay effects, the crown jewel may just be Delay Designer because of the depth of parameter control it offers and the breadth of echo effects that are possible with it.

Delay Designer is a multitap delay. Up to 26 individual taps, or delays, can be fed back into the circuit and can each be edited in very creative ways to make unusual and highly unique delay effects. This large number of taps contributes to the sophistication of the sonic design results that are possible with Delay Designer. The plug-in can be used in mono, stereo, and even surround. While Delay Designer can be used for basic echo effects, the taps can be designed into evolving, pitched, complex rhythms. You'll find some of these within the folders of factor presets that are appropriated labeled Complex, Filtered, and Warped.

A Mini Tour of the Interface

The Main display area of Delay Designer is used to edit the tap parameters. Selecting one of the View buttons on top (Cutoff, Resonance, Transposition, Pan, and Level) determines which parameter is represented in the Main display area for editing.
The Overview display, directly beneath the View buttons in the upper right of the Main display area, conveniently shows all the taps in the timeline in a miniaturized view.

Each tap in the Main display area is a shaded line. The bright bar portion of the tap indicates the value of the active parameter. At the bottom of each tap is an identification letter for each tap—that is, A, B, C, and so on. You can move the taps backward or forward in time and, naturally, create and delete taps. You can create additional taps in three ways: by using the Tap pad, by creating them in the identification bar, or by copying existing taps. At the bottom of the Delay Designer window in the light-blue shaded area is the Tap Parameter bar with the overall levels for Cutoff, Reso, and so on.

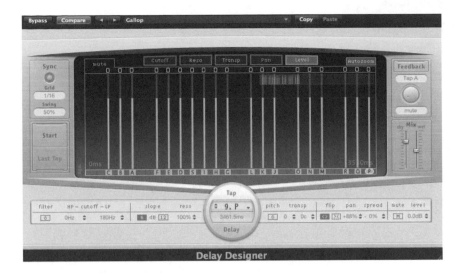

Figure 9.9: Delay Designer

Programming with the Tap Pads

To create taps with the Tap pads, click on the Start pad first, which erases all existing taps. When you tap it once, the label switches from Start to Tap and a red recording bar appears below the View buttons. The taps are created at the time you play them in, as though you were programming drum pads with a specific rhythm in mind. To stop, click on the Last Tap button directly beneath.

If you aren't comfortable tapping in real time, you can create taps by step input in the Identification bar underneath each of the delay taps, where the identification letters are. The letters are based on their order of creation. Tap A was the first tap, Tab B the second tap, and so on. Option-drag to copy a tap. Whichever method of input you choose, the idea is to let yourself experiment with the placement and color of your delay taps and open up fully to the idea of a delay being a sound-design tool.

Figure 9.10: The Tap Pads

Creating Melodies with the Delay Taps

There aren't any other delays that are as simple to use to come up with some really great creative settings quickly for any style of music.

The workspace inside of Delay Designer gives you a horizontal timeline as you pencil in grid markers according to the grid setting on the left. So this example is set to 16th notes. You can set the level for each marker on the timeline when you click on them. You see semitones when you're on the Transposition (pitch) tab so can make it do any melody on the delays.

Each delay tap can have a different pitch or panning, depending what the primary melody of the track wants. It's based on the song, whether it's minor or major. Delay Designer gives you a lot of control over the taps. With other delays I'd have to transpose each piece of audio in Logic's Sample Editor. Delay Designer gives you a quick way to experiment with different settings on the taps.

In this track, the grid is at quarter notes, which makes a dramatic melody. First is labeled "A" underneath the tap, at the bottom of the timeline, and has a semitone value of 1. The second tap is labeled "B" and is set to +5 semitones, the next taps are set to semitones respectively of +8, 6, 5, 6, 3, 5, and 0. You see the semitone value when you click on the tap; that's how you make the adjustment, too. You can create a whole melody out of the taps, just sliding them around until the melody sounds good. This particular song is "dancey dubstep." You can Shift-select the taps on the letters at the bottom and Option-drag them. Just drag up and down to change the semitones.

Whichever delay tap is selected, its value is displayed below at the center of the enlarged circle where it's labeled "Tap Delay." You can see here that Tap E has the semitone value of 5 and where it is in time after the original signal is 2,158.3 ms. Here at the bottom of the interface, I might also adjust the filter cutoff by raising the High Pass (labeled HP) to approximately 400–500 Hz to create a radio effect, but not in this example. The whole section at the bottom displays your overall settings, except for that enlarged center circle showing you the value of the highlighted tap.

You can grab all the taps by swiping across them to trim your setting and that way adjust as a group all your taps. There's a graphic representation preview in the upper right of the whole delay timeline, which is very helpful. If you swipe in the main workspace, you can drag left and right. Sometimes I'll disable the grid when I want an effect of an odd delay. —*Rick Sheppard*

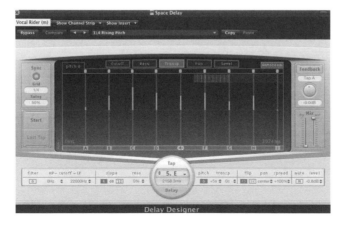

Figure 9.11: Rick Sheppard's setting with pitched delay taps

Match EQ Tricks

This plug-in may well be more for the Logic musician-turned-engineer than a professional engineer who matches EQs in his sleep. I'm a fan of its magic for special circumstances. I've noticed that it is often overlooked mainly because Logic users haven't sorted out exactly what it's for, or how to use it, with the exception of our Logic musician-turned-engineer Greg Kurstin, who is a big fan and has a few unconventional uses for it.

The Match EQ plug-in allows you to "match" and transfer the frequency spectrum from one signal to another. You can also store it as a spectral template file. In this way, you can acoustically match the sound of various songs for an album, or impart the "sound" of any reference source onto your own recordings. Imagine one of these scenarios: vocal overdubs were accidentally recorded with a different microphone than the one used for the main recordings, or the singer shows up for overdubs with a slight cold and is sounding a bit nasal.

The alignment of signals is automatic, but you can also manually draw or modify the filter curve to alter the sound as required. Match EQ acoustically matches two audio signals. It does not, however, match any dynamic differences in the two signals.

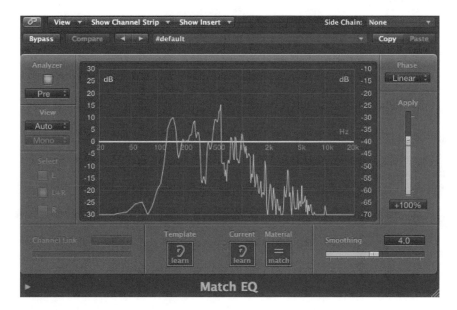

Figure 9.12: The Match EQ

How the Match EQ Works

Match EQ is a learning equalizer that reads the frequency spectrum of any reference source, including the input signal, an audio file, or a template. You can also load a setting file or import the settings of another Match EQ instance via a copy and paste operation. You can analyze the average audio spectrum of the track that the plug-in is assigned to or load another setting file or template. By matching both spectra, a filter curve is generated. This generated curve adapts the track signal to match the sound of the template.

The internal analyzer allows you to visually check the frequency spectrum of the original data and the resulting curve. If required, you can modify the filter curve by boosting or cutting gain in different frequencies, or inverting it.

The Analyzer Display

The View pull-down menu allows you to select the type of information shown on the analyzer display in the center:

- **Template:** The analyzer display shows the average frequency curve, which is generated by analyzing the input signal or loading a template.
- **Current Material:** The analyzer visualizes the average frequency curve, which is generated by analyzing the track signal or loading a Setting file or template.
- **Filter:** The analyzer displays the filter curve, which is generated by matching the Template and the spectra of the Current Material.

The analyzer is enabled with the on/off button. You can select whether the analyzer displays both audio channels via separate curves (L&R) or via the summed maximum level (LR Max). The Template and Current Material buttons perform the spectral analysis of the audio signals, and match the resulting curves.

Template or Current Material Learn Button

Clicking on the Learn button in the Template section starts and stops measurement of the average frequency spectrum in the reference signal. Clicking on the Learn button in the Current Material section starts and stops measurement of the average frequency spectrum in the audio material of the track.

Audio files can also be dragged onto the Template or Current Material Learn buttons to generate template or current spectra. Think of the possibilities! Control-click on either of the Learn buttons and a context menu opens. This menu allows the spectrum of the template or the track signal (Current Material) to be cleared or copied to the Match EQ clipboard, pasted from the Match EQ clipboard to the active instance, or loaded from a stored Setting file. Choose the Generate Template/Current Material Spectrum from the audio file option, and select an appropriate file in the file selector that appears.

Note: When you activate the Learn button in either the Template or Current Material section and the View parameter is set to Auto, the analyzer will display the current status of the spectral analysis, indicated by a progress bar.

The Match Button

The Match button in the Current Material section allows you to write the differences between the learned or loaded Template and the learned or loaded spectrum of the Current Material to a filter curve. Differences in gain are automatically compensated for with the resulting EQ curve referenced to the 0 dB line. The filter curve updates each time a new template or current material spectrum is learned or loaded when the Match button is enabled. You can toggle between the matched filter curve and a flat response by activating/deactivating the Match button.

Each time that a new audio spectrum is matched—either by loading/learning a new spectrum while Match is activated or by activating Match after a new spectrum has been loaded—existing manual modifications are deleted, and Apply is set to 100%.

Only one Learn button can be active at a time. If the Learn button in the Template section is active and you press the Learn button in the Current Material section, the analysis of the template file stops, and the current status is used as the spectral template. Analysis of the track (Current Material) will begin. If you manually modify the filter curve, the original curve can be restored by Option-clicking on the background of the analyzer display. A second Option-click restores the most recently modified curve.

Experiment with this plug-in as soon as possible! Sing into two different microphones or have your singer do so, or sing on two different days when you or your singer are bound to feel and perform a bit differently. Or, drag an audio file of a favorite mix—your own or from another artist—onto the Template or Current Material Learn button and have some fun applying the curve to an audio file in your project.

Real-World Discoveries with Match EQ

Here are the scenarios that producer Greg Kurstin has discovered.

> The Roland Juno 106 had such a great bass frequency that easily fits into a track, so I made a Match EQ setting from the Juno and applied it to a live Fender Bass. I mostly use it when a bass sound doesn't have enough of the "right" kind of low end that I need, like if the bass is too "subby" and isn't punching through the mix. I'll boost the Juno 106 frequencies in the Match EQ and it helps the other bass be more audible, if I'm not hearing enough of the notes of another bass.
>
> Or, I read this somewhere and it's pretty cool: If two things are in the same frequency range, like a keyboard part is in the same range as a vocal, I use the Match EQ almost like a "reverse" match EQ to find the frequency that's the same in both, then pull down its level. I can just take out the frequency of either the keyboard or the vocal that's getting in the way of the other. —*Greg Kurstin*

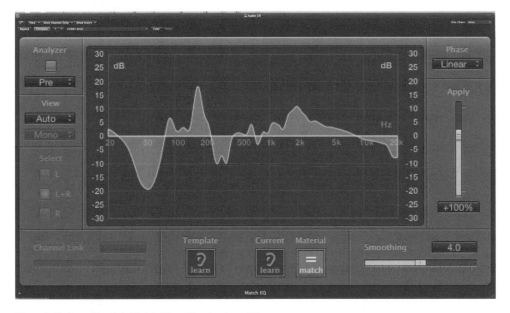

Figure 9.13: Greg Kurstin's Match EQ setting for Juno 106

PART IV: OTHER BASIC STUFF FOR PROS

Chapter 10

GOOD HOUSEKEEPING
(AND OTHER SMART PRACTICES)

Managing Your Logic Project

The assets of a Logic project have become increasingly tidy in every new version since Logic has been an Apple application. The organization of projects and their backups is entirely in line with the file architecture of OS X. Familiarize yourself with first, all the folders for Logic settings in the Application Support root level and home folders, and second, where the assets of a Logic project live and how to import and export from the project—and your Logic life will be a lot smoother.

Managing Your Logic Project Assets

Logic song files are automatically saved into a Logic project folder with all the related assets of the project. The application is trying to direct you to practice good housekeeping and keep everything in one place, including your EXS24 instruments and their associated samples (also the Ultrabeat samples). An extremely common error is to forget to enable the inner checkboxes of the Advanced Options in the assets folder, the result being that the associated samples are not included in the project folder. It is your choice whether to include the samples, but if you keep them in one project folder you will always have those, say, drum samples and violin samples that you need for the song to play back properly on another computer or in another studio. All of your Logic project folders should be backed up in at least two places. That is the best way to ensure that there you'll always have a backup when you need one.

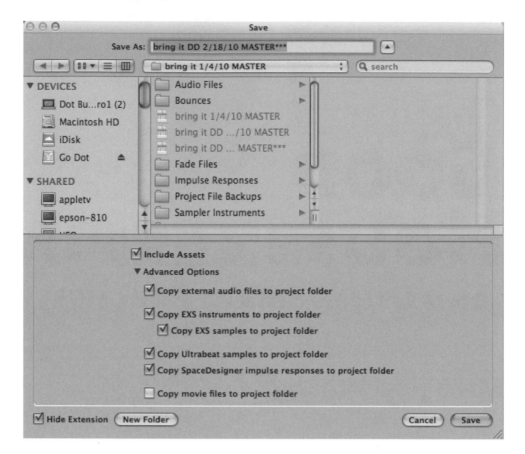

Figure 10.1: The Logic project folder

When viewing from the Finder, the Logic song file is the file in the project folder with an icon of a music keyboard.

📁 Audio Files	▸
🎹 black nail polish DD 2/24/10 master***	
📁 Fade Files	▸
📁 Impulse Responses	▸
📁 Sampler Instruments	▸
📁 Samples	▸
📁 Undo Data	▸

Figure 10.2: Logic song file

Project Templates

Back in the day, there was the Autoload. This was the default Logic song file you created as your starting point for a new Logic project. Logic users spent a lot of time designing their Autoload to include cabling to their external hardware synthesizer.

When software instruments were introduced, many users added to their Autoload a palette of favorite sounds: their favorite acoustic piano, favorite bass sound, favorite drum kit. In fact some professional Logic users had multiple Autoloads, depending on what sort of project they were starting, whether a dance track or a pop song. If you are speaking to a longtime Logic user, he or she is likely to still refer to their default song as an Autoload, but Logic has renamed these as "project templates," to be more generic and encourage the idea that you can have multiple project templates depending on the type of project you are starting. If someone mentions their Autoload, you'll know you're talking to an old timer—so be sure to pick their brain for ancient Logic secrets! There are some great factory templates, like Surround Production or MultiTrack Production, that you may want to check out for different situations. There are also some great templates by musical genre with various software instruments and effects plug-ins preloaded (for example, Electronic or Orchestral) that may provide a good starting point for creating your own project templates.

To create a project template, start with an Empty Project or another factory template, then open whatever instruments or plug-ins, or number of empty audio or software instrument tracks you like to see when you get started, and select from the File menu > Save as Template.

Figure 10.3: Creating a project template

Managing Your Audio Files in the Audio Bin

If you make the Audio Bin your friend in Logic, you will have very organized projects and much fewer headaches. Trust me on this.

Most Logic users have an extremely messy bin of audio files, and it's not entirely their fault. Once you've selected the record path for your audio, the first time you start recording into a project, Logic no longer asks you to set a path so you are not prompted to name a new audio file when you arm a new track to record. Of course, proper recording technique from the days of tape means naming the tracks in your track list before you begin recording, just like labeling leader tape on the console before recording to tape began. When the tracks in the track list are labeled first, audio files are properly named because they take on the name of the track.

Somehow, life inside the DAW encourages some lazy habits. It's easy to end up with a bunch of audio files in the Bin that have a generic name: Audio 1_1, Audio 1_2, etc. To rename in the Bin, click on the audio file name and enter the new name. The file names visible from the Finder are now updated.

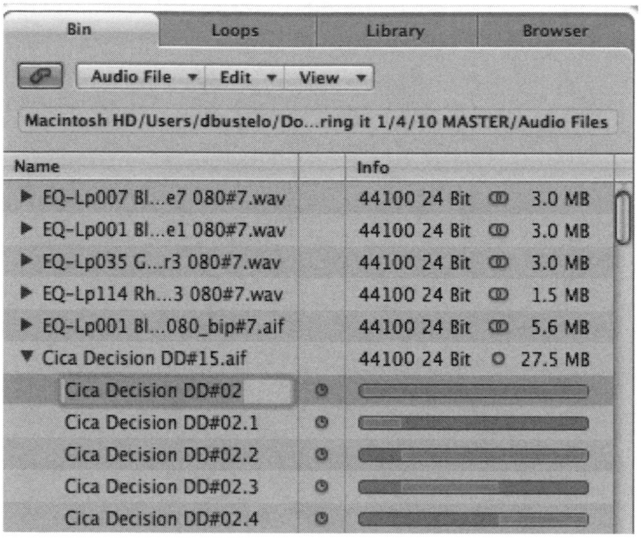

Figure 10.4: Renaming audio files in the Bin

This is distinct from the feature in the Arrange window that allows you to transfer the audio track name to the regions visible in the Arrange window. This does not update the audio file names that will be visible in the Finder if you need to search!

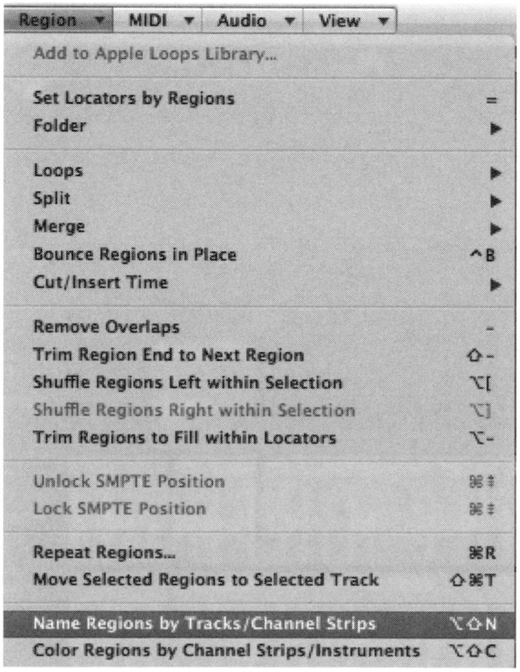

Figure 10.5: Renaming regions in the Arrange window by track name

Optimizing audio files is another useful option in the Audio Bin for removing the dead space on an audio file in order to reduce the file size. While hard-drive space is cheap, there are obvious advantages to a Logic project folder being as compact as possible, whether to squeeze it onto a portable drive that's jam-packed or to save on upload time when sharing files over iChat, iDisk, or other file-sharing servers.

To optimize an audio file in the Audio Bin, do the following:

- Choose Edit > Select Used menu.
- Choose Audio File > Optimize File(s).
- Logic determines the file segments not contained in regions used in the Arrange window and deletes them.

The function uses a one-second pre-roll and post-roll. Special note: There is no undo for this function!

Track Import

From the Browser tab in the Media area of the Arrange window, you can navigate to any Logic project to import elements from it. When you find the project folder, double-click on the Logic song file within it. Once the project is visible in the Browser view, you will see a complete table of all the assets from that project—that is, audio tracks, software instrument tracks, and even auxiliary tracks. Here, you can enable and disable any of the tracks and their associated components, and then select on the bottom to add or replace that track in the Arrange workspace—in other words, you can take everything or take one individual component like the plug-in chain or MIDI data.

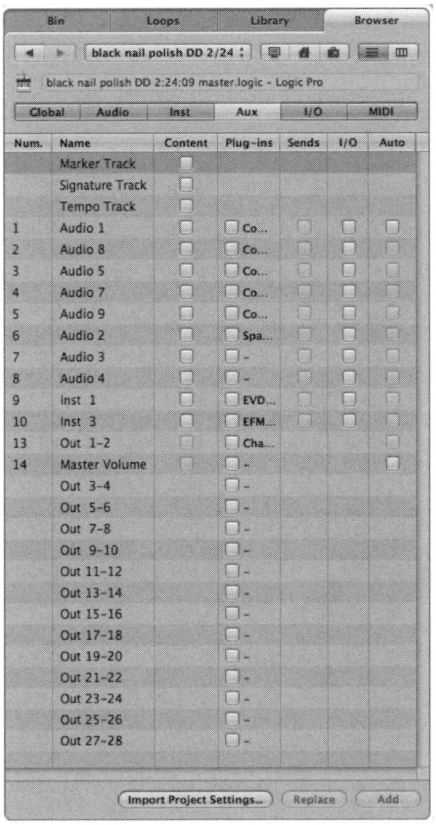

Figure 10.6: Track Import view

There are two rows of labels in the Track Import view. The row of tabs on top refers to the type of track—whether audio, instrument, auxiliary, MIDI, and so on. This allows you to focus on which tracks you need to import if you're working on a large project. The columns beneath are labeled in the Track Import view as follows:

- **Track Number:** The track numbers in the track list of the Arrange window.
- **Track Name:** The track names as labeled in the track list of the Arrange window.
- **Content:** The MIDI or audio data contained on a selected track. These can be imported independently of the plug-in chain on the track.
- **Plug-ins:** Self-explanatory; the entire plug-in chain from a track, including third-party plug-ins.
- **Sends:** The bus assignments on the Sends. This field is grayed out if there are no Send assignments.
- **Auto:** The automation data on the track.

Note: You cannot import track data from an open Logic project. Logic does allow you to have more than one project open at a time, so you may accidentally catch yourself trying to import data from a project that's open!

Backing Up Your Presets and Settings

Any settings that you create in Logic—such as channel strip settings, plug-in settings, or Space Designer IRs—are placed in the Logic folder in the Application Support folder of your Home folder. This Logic folder should be backed up, and of course that means backed up in two places, for safekeeping. This is also the folder you will want to keep consistent between all of your computers so that you always have all your plug-in settings.

This file path should become very familiar to you.

Figure 10.7: Your Logic folder in the Finder

Bounce and Export Settings

The Bounce and Export settings in Logic are quite detailed and self-explanatory, but worth mentioning here so you are aware of all the great options.

Bouncing a Master File

Logic nailed it with the bounce options. You access the Bounce menu from either the bottom of the main output channel strip of the File menu (File > Bounce) or the Bounce tool in the toolbar. All three bring up the same dialog box. In the Bounce menu you can select between real time and offline. Real time is obviously faster at no loss of quality. Offline makes sense if you don't need to hear the final mix another time and would prefer to rest your ears.

The bounces by default are placed in a Bounce folder within the Logic project folder. In the Bounce dialog box, you are free to redirect the path to anywhere on your hard drive. You may prefer to keep all your bounces in one location, for example.

In the Bounce dialog box, you can also choose to create simultaneously an MP3 with a checkbox to send directly to your iTunes library, which is pretty awesome. And you can also burn directly to a CD. Burning a CD requires a real-time bounce and cannot be done during an offline bounce.

Bounce in Place

You can select to bounce in place an individual region or an entire track from the local region and track menus in the Arrange window for any highlighted region or track. The dialog box that opens is quite detailed, allowing you to choose whether to create a new track and mute the original or replace it. You also have the choice to include or not include any effects plug-ins on the track.

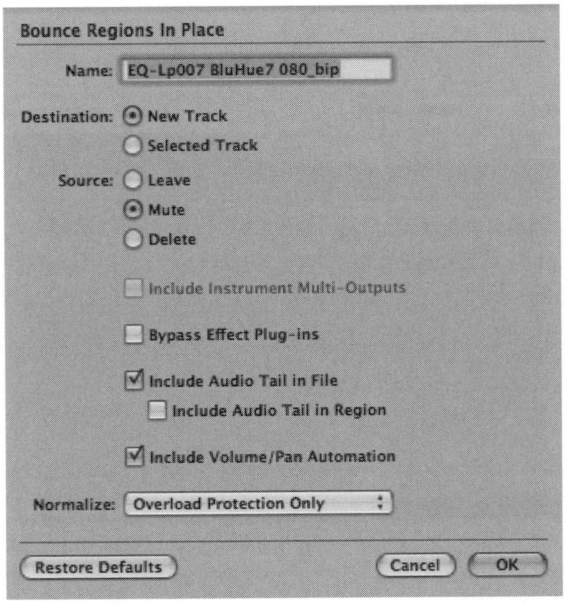

Figure 10.8: Bounce in place

Track Export

If a band or producer is delivering Logic stems for you to mix, or as the musician you are delivering to an engineer, Logic has great options for exporting audio. From the File menu in the Arrange window, select the Export menu. Then choose either Export Track As Audio File or All Tracks As Audio Files. This will create a complete audio stem (or stems), beginning at the top of the song and continuing until the end. Any separate regions on the track(s) will be combined into new continuous audio file(s).

You can access the same Export menu by Control-clicking or right-clicking directly on the audio file.

Figure 10.9: Track Export menu

Power Tip: Exporting Tracks with Plug-Ins on Main Outs

The Export function in Logic keeps all plug-ins, unless you Option-click to bypass them. However, it zeros out the volumes, which is a much-debated choice for the default. The rationale is that tracks are being exported in order to be mixed on another system, which of course is not always the case.

Power Tip: When Bouncing in Place

If the bounce seems to be a bit late, check if there are any plug-ins on the main output. You will want to do this even when the plug-in delay compensation is set to All in your audio preferences (Preferences > Audio > General). Plug-ins on the main output cannot be compensated, so be sure to manually bypass before the bounce in place.

Key Commands: The Secret to Learning Logic (condensed)

An entire chapter was devoted to this subject in *The Power in Logic Pro*, so consider it a very important topic and, this condensed version not to be taken lightly. Key commands are the essence of both learning Logic and working with speed and efficiency as a power Logic user. Give yourself adequate time to explore this vast universe of over 1,000 Logic keyboard shortcuts.

To access the Key Commands window, go to the Preference button in the toolbar and select Key Commands from the bottom of the list. Or, open the window from the default key command, Option + K.

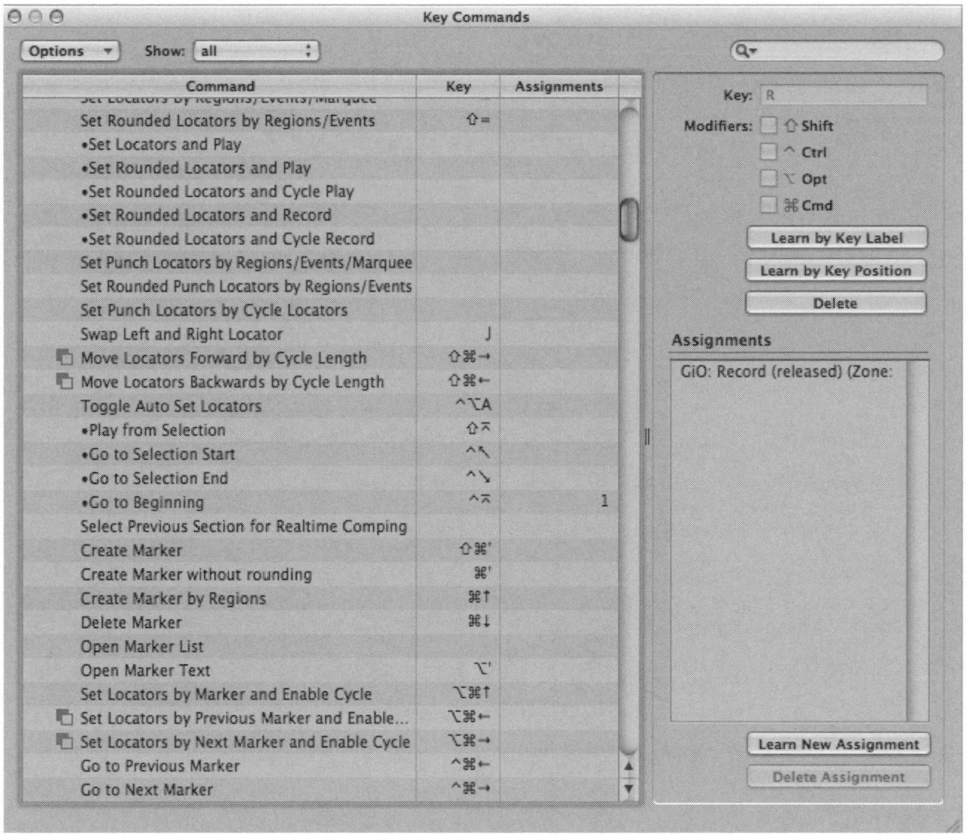

Figure 10.10: The Key Commands window

Below is a quick list of the highlights of using key commands to dramatically improve your engineering workflow in Logic.

Creating Custom Key Commands

To modify an existing key command, enable the button Learn by Key Label, on the right. Next, use the search field in the upper right to navigate to the function you want to assign a keystroke to. Then, select a key combination using a letter key with (or without) a modifier key.

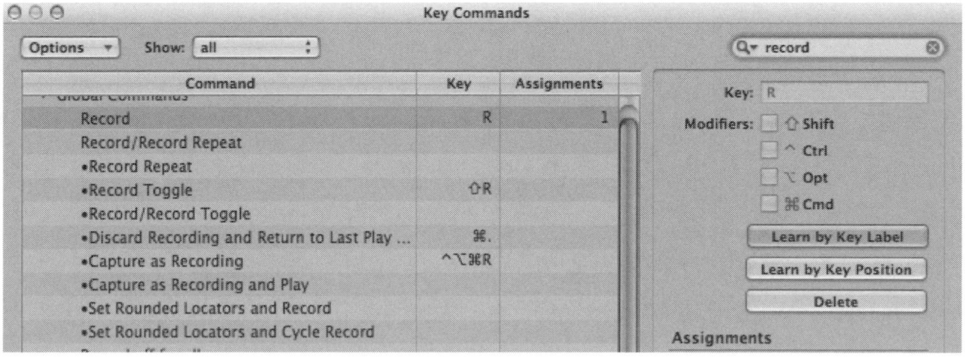

Figure 10.11: Assigning a key command

If the key combination is already in use, a dialog box will pop up telling you what the keystroke was previously assigned to. You'll have the option to override and replace its assignment or find another key combination.

Finding Out What a Shortcut Is Assigned To

Simply press the key or combination of keys, and the shortcut it is assigned to will be brought into view and highlighted. You must be inside the Key Commands window to perform this test. Be sure that nothing is typed into the search field in the upper right of your screen or this won't work!

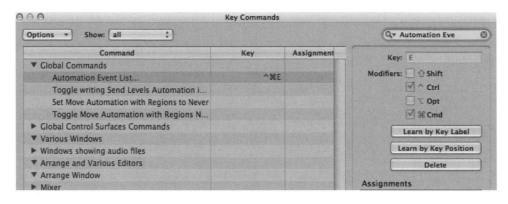

Figure 10.12: Finding an existing key command assignment

Loading and Saving Key Command Sets

You can access different key command sets from within the Key Commands window. This means that you can carry your own set around to load in another studio.

To load another key command set, select the Options menu in the upper left of the Key Commands window. Here, you will find the factory presets, including key commands in different languages. There is also a Pro Tools key command set that you may or may not find helpful if you are a Pro Tools user. Since many functions have different names in the two DAWs, the translation is a bit inexact.

Beneath the presets is the option to import and export your own key command set.

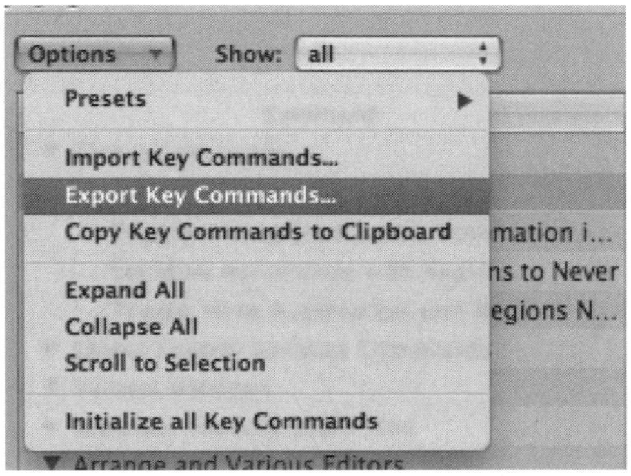

Figure 10.13: Export menu for your key commands

To save your customized key commands, use the Export function and they will be automatically saved to the Key Commands subfolder within the Logic folder of your Home Folder.

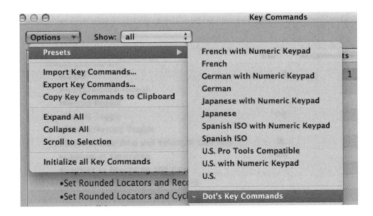

Figure 10.14: File Path in Finder to key commands

Once you've created your own custom set, it will appear under the presets in the Key Commands window below the divider line. If you are bringing your custom set to another studio, use the Import Key Commands menu to navigate to your portable drive.

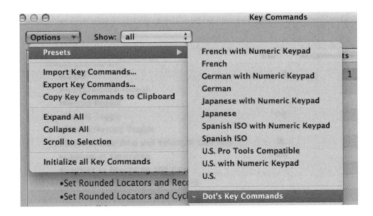

Figure 10.15: Dot's custom key commands

Printing (and Memorizing) the Key Commands

Under Options select Copy Key Commands to Clipboard, and then open Microsoft Word or another text-edit application. Next select Paste or Command + V, and the key commands will be pasted into a document that you can now print.

Before you copy to the clipboard, you may want to limit the Key Commands view to just the ones that are assigned. This option is labeled "Used" in the Select menu to the right. Otherwise, the document you print out may be quite lengthy to accommodate over 1,000 key commands!

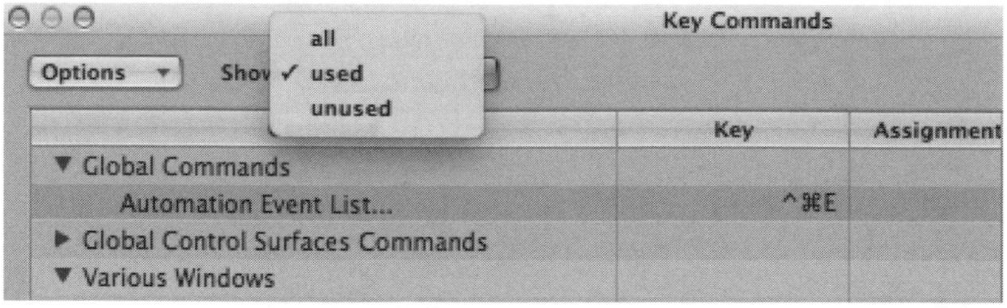

Figure 10.16: Select used key commands

If you forget which symbol refers to the various modifier keys like Control or Option on the QWERTY keyboard, there is a table in the upper right of the Key Commands window.

Power Tip: Protecting Your Key Commands

A common troubleshooting recommendation when Logic is acting buggy is to trash your Logic preferences. However, the key commands are stored in the Logic Preference file. They won't be deleted from your hard drive, but you'll have to reload them from the Preset window. To avoid this extra step, under Preferences in the toolbar of the Arrange window, there is an option to initialize all preferences except your key commands (Preferences > Initialize All Except Key Commands).

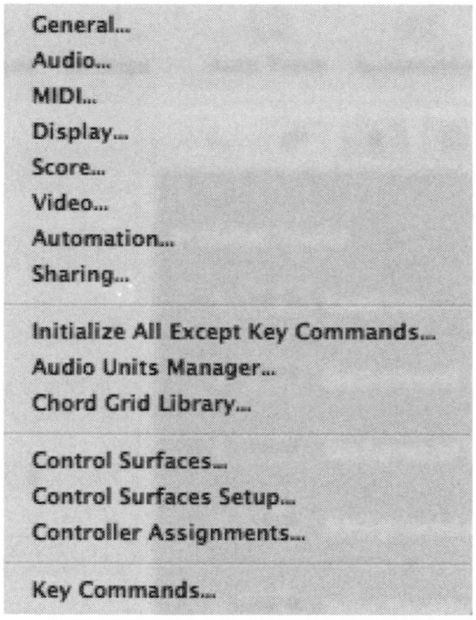

Figure 10.17: Initializing preferences except your key commands

Dot's Favorite Key Commands

Over the years, many Logic users watching me work have asked me to send them the list that is shared in appendix A, "Dot's Favorite Key Commands." Cross-reference in the book any terminology and features you are not familiar with. Start your own hot list of key commands to commit to memory, along with any of mine that you find relevant to your workflow.

Your key command list should be a living document that you update and reference regularly, especially at the beginning when you're first learning Logic. You'll find that you will need to refine your key command list with every new version of Logic since new key commands are introduced relevant to new features, which sometimes bumps former preset assignments.

Staying Organized and Tidy

Logic projects can quickly become massive sessions with literally hundreds of audio and software instrument tracks given the high audio track count possible in Logic. Making the effort early on to develop good organizational habits will make these larger sessions more manageable and allow you to always work fast and efficiently regardless of the project size.

Making Notes in Your Project

This is a cool, relatively new feature in Logic. You can keep a text file within the project for any mix notes about the plug-in settings used, mix levels, the different vocal takes still under consideration, and so on.

You create notes from the Notes tool in the toolbar on the upper right of the Arrange window. When you select Notes, there are two tabs to choose from: "Project," which will be global for the project, and "Track," which is for an individual track. The Notes window allows you to pick even the font and the font size.

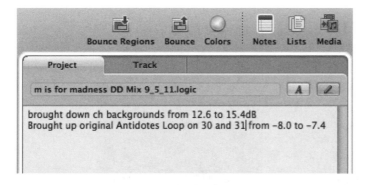

Figure 10.18: Project notes

You can also create notes directly in the Mixer underneath each channel strip (Mixer > View > Notes).

I/O Labels

While you're labeling and making everything tidy in your Logic project, keep in mind that you can label the objects in the Mixer—such as Inputs, Outputs, Auxes, and Buses—with the I/O Labels (Mixer > Options > I/O Labels).

Markers Complete Your Project

Markers are the key to keeping an arrangement well organized, and they are a brilliant navigational tool. These are your visual road map of the Logic project arrangement. Markers are generally used to designate the main structural sections of a Logic project: for example, Introduction, Verse, Chorus, Verse 2, Bridge, Chorus 2, Break, Chorus Out, Ending, and so on.

There are key commands to jump to the next and previous markers. For any Pro Tools users who are reading now, there are key commands to Go to Previous/Next Marker and Go to Marker Number just as in Pro Tools. Beyond the increased speed you'll experience in your navigation of a project, you will find markers a great tool for staying focused and on top of the project arrangement at a glance.

Creating Markers in the Global Tracks

Global tracks are, just as they sound, specialized tracks in Logic that contain data that applies uniformly to all the audio and MIDI tracks. The global tracks are found at the top of the track list, with a small disclosure triangle that opens the view to the various global tracks. Click on the global tracks to reveal the Marker track.

Figure 10.19: Global tracks

Now click on the disclosure triangle next to the Marker track to open up the full view of creating, naming, and editing your Marker track.

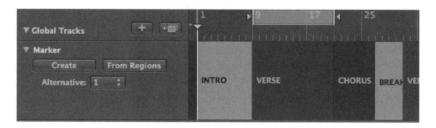

Figure 10.20: Marker track

Move the playhead to the point at which you'd like to create a marker, and press the Create button in the Marker track header field.

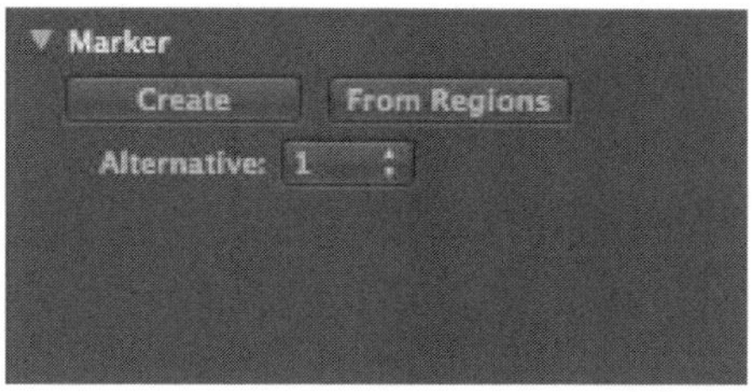

Figure 10.21: Create Marker button

You can adjust the start and end points of the marker by dragging on it. The Pointer tool turns into a bracket-shaped tool to make adjustments to the marker length, once you have at least two markers in the Marker track.

Double-click into the marker to change its name from the default of Marker 1, Marker 2, and so on.

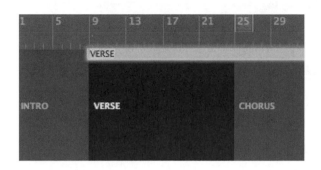

Figure 10.22: Naming markers

Cycle by Marker

There are great ways to navigate quickly by your markers. As mentioned above, there are key commands that can be assigned to Go To Next Marker and Go To Previous Marker so you can quickly jump from Verse 1 to Chorus 2 and by marker number. When Cycle is enabled in the transport and the Marker track is in view in the global tracks, simply drag up on the marker into the bar ruler and the Marker area will become the cycle area.

View Markers in Bar Ruler

After the Marker track is created, you can leave it in view or collapse it and the markers will remain visible but smaller inside the bottom half of the bar ruler. You can't cycle by marker if the Marker track isn't in view, but you can use the key commands to fly between the markers.

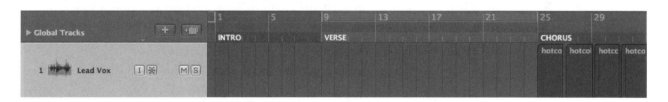

Figure 10.23: The Marker view in the bar ruler

Coloring Markers

Option + C will open the same color palette used for coloring tracks. Or, select the color palette in the toolbar.

Simply click on the marker with your Pointer tool so that it's highlighted, then select the color you'd like to assign from the color palette.

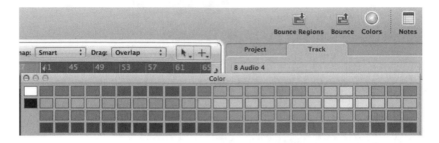

Figure 10.24: The color palette

I Just Updated My OS and Logic Is Crashing !

I thought that everyone already knew this one, but I recently got a phone call from a producer friend with a number of major label credits and guess what happened? He just upgraded his operating system to Lion, and Logic is crashing all the time. He didn't know what I'm about to share, so here goes for anyone else who might not yet know this Apple axiom: the likelihood that an Apple application would be the culprit for causing a hard crash when Apple upgrades the operating system is highly unlikely.

I don't like to point fingers, but when there's a hard crash in Logic, there's no choice. It is likely that you have something third party that is not yet compatible with the new operating system. It could be your external hardware that needs an update, so quickly check the manufacturer website for your audio and MIDI interfaces. Otherwise, it's likely that one of your plug-ins needs an OS update. The quick and drastic way to test is to remove all your plug-ins and see if the crash reoccurs. If it doesn't, the next step is to sort out who the bad guy is. I would start by adding back in any essential plug-ins or, conversely, remove any plug-ins you rarely use. As with the hardware, do a quick check online on manufacturer websites or forums if others have reported the problem or if an update is available. You don't need to delete the plug-ins—just move them out of the path that Logic will look to.

Know the Components Folder

If you have recurring problems with your Logic studio, there is a good chance that they could be emanating from third-party plug-ins. Third-party plug-ins recognized by Logic are of the Audio Unit format. Logic does not support VSTs since the Apple OS X operation system was introduced. Audio Units are installed globally and will work once they are installed in both Logic and GarageBand, as well as in many other Mac-based applications. Audio Units live on your hard drive in the Components folder.

Audio Units may be in the Components folder at either the root level of your computer or in your Home folder: /Library/Audio/Plug-Ins/Components or ~/Library/Audio/Plug-Ins/Components. (Note: "~" represents your home directory.)

I would start by removing from the Components folder (Library > Audio > Plug-Ins > Components) any Audio Units that you are not using. To remove, just drag them to the desktop or create another safe folder for them on the same directory level, and call them something like "Unused Components" or "X-Components." When you want to use one of them again, just slide it back into the original location in the Components folder.

You don't need to do anything drastic immediately and remove them all, but keep that option open if nothing else helps. At that point, remove all of them and then add them back one by one until you can reproduce the crashing. This can be time-consuming but effective.

Make sure that plug-ins are updated from their respective manufacturer websites. This naturally applies only to legitimate plug-ins that you have purchased. Keep in mind that any troubleshooting and compatibility problem solving applies to legitimate products only. No QA or technical-support teams are testing cracks!

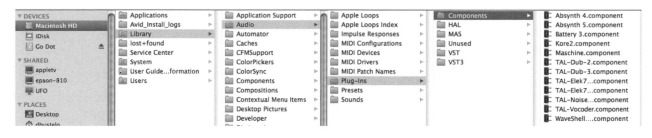

Figure 10.25: Components view from Finder

Creating Versus Engineering

It might seem an arbitrary delineation that my first book on Logic Pro, *The Power in Logic Pro*, was about creating and this book is about engineering. Engineering is creative and integral to every stage of the creative process. In the new world of working in a DAW, there may not even be a separate mixing stage, and mixing is in large part achieved as many musicians and producers work. The lines are certainly blurred. Musicians are producers, producers are engineers, and many good recording engineers are musicians by training, which means that they can just hear when something is out of tune, or what key a song is in, or whether there should be an electronic kick sound blended in with the live drummer. Is the individual who performs drum replacement/doubling—and creates the instrumentation for the most important element in the track—engineering, or creating?

All caveats aside, there is something to be said for tackling the topics and problem solving in Logic that would most interest a professional engineer and the musician finding him or herself in that role. Your assignment now is to experiment with all these tools as often and as soon as possible! Your increased speed and appreciation of the Logic workflow as the engineer or producer will hopefully make the creative process that much more enjoyable for everyone in the studio.

Appendix A: Dot's Key Commands in Logic

Here are the Logic key commands that substantially speed up my personal workflow. These were not default assignments, but ones that felt "logical" to me. So, I customized the keystroke combinations. See chapter 10 for further information about the following:

- Getting instructions regarding how to customize your own key commands
- Finding out what a keystroke combination is assigned to
- Learning how to load, save, and print selected sets of key commands.
- Study the Key Commands window and the Logic terminologies contained therein (often, it helps to cross-reference with the Help Files), and then create your own hot list of essential key commands. Carry them with you and commit them to memory.

1. Record	Return
2. Go to Position	G
3. Go to Next Marker	Shift + M
4. Go to Previous Marker	Option + M
5. Mute Region	M
6. Solo Region	S
7. Capture as Recording	Shift + R
8. Record Toggle (drop into Play mode)	Command + R
9. Play or Stop	Spacebar
10. Cycle Mode	C
11. Lock/Unlock Current Screenset	Shift + L
12. Show Tools	Escape
13. Next Channel Strip or Plug-In Setting or EXS Instrument	N
14. Previous Channel Strip or Plug-In Setting or EXS Instrument	P
15. Open Color Palette	Option + C
16. Hide/Show Track Automation	A
17. Repeat Regions	R
18. Forward (by one bar)	Right Arrow
19. Rewind (by one bar)	Left Arrow
20. Zoom Horizontal Out	Option + Right Arrow
21. Zoom Horizontal In	Option + Left Arrow
22. Open Key Commands	Option + K
23. Loop Regions	L
24. Convert Loops to Real Copies	Control + L
25. Create Trackname	Shift + N
26. Select Next Track	Down Arrow
27. Select Previous Track	Up Arrow
28. Create Marker	Command + M
29. Toggle Group Clutch	Shift + G
30. Toggle Zoom to Fit Selection (Select All first)	Z

Note: Here's one more essential move worth memorizing: Select a region and then press Control + Shift to disconnect from the beat grid. This lets you slide the region freely along the timeline, and nudge by the smallest increment.

APPENDIX B: LOGIC PRO TERMINOLOGY AND PRESET U.S. KEY COMMANDS* FOR PRO TOOLS ENGINEERS

*There are two sets of U.S. presets: one with the numeric keypad on the QWERTY keyboard, and one without. If not indicated otherwise under the column Logic Without Numeric Keypad, the key command is the same.

Presets are accessed in the Key Commands window (Arrange > Preferences > Key Commands > Options > Presets). See the section "Key Commands: The Secret to Learning Logic (condensed)," in chapter 10, for steps to search and make custom assignments in the Key Commands window.

Additional Note: Starting with Pro Tools 10, the term *Clip* replaces *Region*.

Transport/Navigation/Zoom

Pro Tools/Task	Logic with Numeric Keypad	Logic Without Numeric
Play	Enter	Shift + Return
Play or Stop	Spacebar	
Stop	0 (numeric keypad)	Return
Pause	. (numeric keypad)	Option + Return
Record	*	R
Play from Selection	Shift + Enter	Shift + Return
Go to Beginning	Return	Ctrl + Return
Go to Position	/ (numeric keypad)	/
Create Marker	Shift + Command + '	
Go to Next Marker	Ctrl + Command + Right Arrow	
Go to Previous Marker	Ctrl + Command + Left Arrow	
Cycle mode	/ (numeric keypad)	C
Define Cycle Range	Click-and-drag lower half bar ruler	
Toggle through tracks in track list	Up Arrow/Down Arrow	
Rewind	,	
Fast Rewind	Shift + ,	
Forward	.	
Fast Forward	Shift + . (numeric keypad)	
Audio Bin	B	
Mixer	X	
Event Editor	E	

Tempo List	T	
Sample (Waveform) Editor	W	
Piano Roll Editor	P	
Zoom tool	Ctrl + Option + lasso selection	
Zoom Horizontal In	Ctrl + Option + Right Arrow	
Zoom Horizontal Out	Ctrl + Option + Left Arrow	
Zoom Vertical In	Ctrl + Option + Down Arrow	
Zoom Vertical Out	Ctrl + Option + Up Arrow	
Zoom to Fit Selection	Z	
Zoom back out	Ctrl + Option-click in background Arrange window	
Auto Zoom (selected track)	Ctrl + Z	

Editing/Arranging

Pro Tools/Task	Logic with Numeric Keypad	Logic Without Numeric
Delete selection	Delete	
Mute/unmute selection (clip)	M	
Merge regions	Ctrl + = (numeric keypad)	Ctrl + =
Split by playhead	\	
Repeat regions/ events	Command + R	
Loop clip	L	
Nudge left	Option + Left Arrow	
Nudge right	Option + Right Arrow	
Delete Fade	Option-click with Crossfade tool	
Adjust Fade Curve	Ctrl + Shift-drag with Crossfade tool	
Strip Silence	Ctrl + X	
Pack Folder	Shift + Command + F	
Toggle Take Folder Quick Swipe Comping	Option + Q	
Scrub Rewind, Scrub Forward	No default assignments	

Mixer and Automation

Pro Tools/Task	Logic with Numeric Keypad	Logic Without Numeric
Mixer	X	
Move Plug-In	Command-drag	
Copy Plug-In	Option + Command-drag	
Solo Safe	Ctrl-click Solo	
Add Track to a Group	Option-click in group field on channel strip	
Group Clutch (disable group)	Command + G	
Open Group Settings	Option + Command + G	
View Automation	A	
Insert node	Click into line	
Delete node	Click on node	
Select node(s)	Shift + lasso selection	
Curves	Ctrl + Option-drag	
Offline Trim	Command-drag automation fader	
Copy-Convert	Option + click-and-hold while selecting another parameter in menu	

Automation Parameter

Pro Tools/Task	Logic with Numeric Keypad	Logic Without Numeric
Automation Modes: Read, Write, Touch, Off	Shift + Ctrl + Command + R, W, T, O, respectively	

Miscellaneous

Pro Tools/Task	Logic with Numeric Keypad	Logic Without Numeric
New Project	Command + N	
New Tracks	Option + Command + N	
Duplicate Track	Command + D	
Key Commands window	Option + K	
Capture as Recording	Ctrl + *	Ctrl + Option + Command + R

Windows and Tools

Pro Tools/Task	Logic with Numeric Keypad	Logic Without Numeric
Edit window	Arrange window	
Mix window	Mixer window	
Clip List	Audio Bin	
I/O Labels	Mixer window > Options > I/O Labels	
Digibase	No database; use Spotlight to search project assets.	

Grabber tool	Pointer tool	
Separation Grabber tool	Pointer tool on marquee selection or Scissors tool	
Trimmer tool	Pointer tool on region start and end	
Loop Trimmer tool	Pointer tool on upper right corner of region	
Smart tool	Pointer tool combines Grabber, Trimmer, and Loop Trimmer tools; for Selector tool functionality, assign Marquee tool as the Command-click tool.	
Selector tool	Marquee tool	
Scrubber tool	Solo tool	
Pencil tool	Pencil tool	
Zoomer tool	Zoom tool; select by holding Ctrl + Option (see above).	
Time Expansion/ Trimmer tool	Option + Pointer tool while changing region length	

Modes and General Functionality

Pro Tools/Task	Logic with Numeric Keypad	Logic Without Numeric
Session file	Project file	
Loop Playback	Cycle	
Heal Separated Clips	Merge (use the Merge tool or the key command Ctrl + =)	
Fade Files folder	A file at the same folder level as a project file	
SMPTE Session Start Time	SMPTE offset	
Sync point	Anchor (edit in Sample Editor or Audio Bin)	
Suspend all Groups	Group Clutch (Mixer > Options > Group Clutch) or key command	
Sync Point	Anchor	
Shuffle mode	Shuffle + L or Shuffle + R (Drag menu)	
Grid mode	Continuous Grid mode; set value in Snap menu	
Absolute and Relative Grid	Relative Grid defaults; Snap > Snap to Absolute Value	
Spot mode	Event Float window displays position and length of selected region or MIDI note (Option + E)	
Loop Playback	Cycle button on transport bar	

Link Timeline & Edit Selection	Play From Selection (Shift + Enter)	
Destructive Recording	No equivalent; a recording is a new audio file.	
Tab-to-Transient	Marquee tool-select, then Right and Left aArrows adjust selection end point, snapping to transients. Shift + Left/ Right Arrows for left selection border; Shift + Home/End shifts selection left/right, respectively.	
Playlists (track based)	Take folders (region based)	
Voices	Maximum number of audio channels is 255. Note: You can have multiple audio tracks with the same channel strip allowing more tracks than the maximum number of audio channels.	
Clip grouping	Folders will move/edit regions as one object (Region > Folder > Pack Folder or Shift + Cmd + F).	
Active and inactive items	To control what is in view and CPU resources: Use Mute Regions to take "offline", no resources used during playback. (Preferences > Audio > General > Track Mute/Solo > "CPU Saving"); Mute/Solo in Arrange window will be less responsive than in Mixer. "Hide/ Unhide tracks" temporarily hides selected tracks but does not reduce processing.	

APPENDIX C: THE DVD-ROM VIDEO TUTORIALS

The accompanying DVD-ROM contains 13 video tutorials designed to assist you in your reading of *Logic Pro for Recording Engineers and Producers*. They provide additional insights into some of the editing tools and mixing techniques covered in the text, along with a real-time glimpse into a fast and efficient Logic workflow.

- Tutorials 1 through 10 cover navigation and editing techniques introduced in the book's Part II, "The Anatomy of Editing in Logic."
- Tutorials 11 through 13 illustrate techniques from Part III, "Mixing in Logic."

Tutorials 1 through 2: Playback in Logic, Parts 1 and 2

The fundamentals of playing back in Logic are covered in Parts 1 and 2:

- Part 1 introduces basic playback from the top of the project or from a specific location.
- Part 2 provides more advanced playback options, including by key command, as well as overriding the cycle selection with the bar ruler or with the powerful single-pixel marquee playback.

Tutorial 3: Zooming Techniques in Logic

Several more basic navigation concepts are covered in this tutorial, including the Zoomer tool, the best key commands for zooming, and other new zoom techniques.

Tutorials 4 through 5: Key Commands, Part 1 "Making Basic Assignments and Key Commands," and Part 2, "Advanced Features"

Insights are presented in this tutorial to help you do the following:

- Navigate the Key Commands window
- Modify existing key command assignments
- Import, export, and print key command sets

Also covered is a power tip for protecting your key commands when deleting your Logic Preferences files for trouble shooting purposes.

Tutorial 6: Hiding Tracks You Don't Need to See

Discover this handy navigation tool that's popular with engineers for editing and mixing. It is especially convenient for hiding tracks in the Arrange window when you are working on larger projects.

Tutorial 7 through 8: The Sample Editor

- Part 1—An Intro
- Part 2—Editing Transients

Part 1 is an introduction to navigation in the Sample Editor and the available types of editing and audio processing. Part 2 focuses on transient editing for situations such as creating effective EXS24 sampler instruments and adjusting vocal timing for remixes.

Tutorial 9 through 10: Beat Mapping, Part 1, and Beat Mapping, Part 2

These easy steps will help you retain a human feel while creating a tempo map for a live performance or sample that was recorded without referencing a click track. Part 1 sets up your basic understanding of the Beat Mapping track in the global tracks. Part 2 completes the introduction to this powerful technique and shows you how to double-check your results and view the resulting map in the Tempo List.

Tutorial 11: The Pro Workflow of Channel Strip Settings

Learn how to create, manage, and navigate through your own channel strip settings for easy access to custom plug-in chains of software instruments, audio tracks, and mastering settings.

Tutorial 12: Tour of the Mixer

Get an essential introduction to the Logic mixer from this tutorial, including the following:

- The Single, Arrange, and All mode buttons
- Other navigation buttons used for isolating the view by track type
- Options for introducing a Mixer channel strip to the Arrange window, and when this may be necessary
- Other mixing features assignable by control-clicking on a channel strip

Tutorial 13:
Power Tips for Mixing in Logic

This tutorial demonstrates a number of important tips for working efficiently in the Logic mixer, such as the following:

- Color-coding track names
- Creating temporary track groups
- Creating and disabling track groups and the group settings
- Making mono and stereo track assignment
- Bypassing plug-ins
- Understanding the Pan Law setting
- Setting up Solo Safe
- Navigating quickly to bus destination channels
- Adjusting the waveform size
- Rearranging plug-ins with the Hand tool

INDEX

About Dot Bustelo

"I think the book will be very helpful to guys like me, who see the benefits of being bilingual in Pro Tools and Logic. What I've read so far gives me three ways to learn Logic: 1) the more detailed how-tos and whys, but with simple, no-fuss language, 2) real-world tips by working experts (the interviews), and 3) the appendices, which [are] a great reference for the functions and nomenclature in Logic that directly correspond with those in Pro Tools, which I work in daily and probably know a bit better. I think for me it now comes down to practice. I just have to be disciplined and set aside some time each day.

I'm about two-thirds of the way through [the book], and I honestly don't have much to say other than "Thank you!" The right-to-the-point approach makes it easy to read and should get the reader going in Logic quickly and without fuss. The interviews are "friendly" and conversational, and I can't wait for the appendices, with [Dot's] favorite key commands and Pro Tools equivalents! I know you can create your own key commands in Logic, but it helps to have a go-to list for reference (especially for Logic dummies like me!)."

— Phil Tan, *multi-Grammy-winning engineer*

"When you got a Logic problem
Dot has wrote a book to solv'em...
And this right hear is it. Yeya!"

—Chad Hugo, *N.E.R.D., The Neptunes*

"Dot Bustelo has been exceptionally helpful in my experience of learning and using Logic. She understands how the artist thinks and always has new tricks to teach."

—A-trak, *DJ/turntablist*

"Dot has made Logic, well, logical. Her approach to teaching is creative and tailored, less from the perspective of a program developer and more so [from] that of a musician and composer."

—Ronnie Vannucci, *The Killers*

"Dot has provided me with an incredible source of in-depth and practical knowledge of Apple's Logic program. She has shown me tricks and tips that have opened creative doors that I didn't even know existed. She has dedicated herself to the absolute mastery of her craft, and is willing to share that wealth of knowledge with the rest of us. Dot Bustelo is quite simply one of the best teachers around."

— Nathaniel Motte, *3OH!3*

"Dot Bustelo has hands-down the most extensive working knowledge of Logic and all its intricacies; I've asked her questions before, and she's able to mentally scroll through the various menus and folders in her head … leaving me to only assume she and Logic have actually become 'one' entity, which is pretty cool."

— Ryan Tedder, *OneRepublic*

"Dot was the first one to introduce me to Logic software, and she has been a valuable resource of information ever since. She knows this software inside and out, and breaks everything down in an easy-to-understand way. And, she knows the best insider techniques that will make your recording more efficient and creative.

Logic is an extremely powerful creative tool, and Dot knows how to get the most out of it. I wonder when Dot will get sick of me asking her Logic-related questions?"

— James Valentine, *Maroon 5*

"My experience with Dot Bustelo and her inspiring Logic tutorials turned me into a Logic user for life. She has a knack for enticing you with her crafty shortcuts that stimulate a deeper understanding of how deep the creative rabbit hole actually is built within Logic as a complete music-production software.

I have had the pleasure of seeing her perform her demos live many times over the years in different settings. I always leave feeling excited to get working on my own songs and implement the new tricks, as the logic within Logic takes hold in my own engineering. Dot enchants as she clarifies precisely how to use Logic, and has always kept her tutorials fresh and fun. Thank you, Dot!"

— DJ Empress

quick PRO

guides *series*

Producing Music with Ableton Live
by Jake Perrine
Softcover w/DVD-ROM •
978-1-4584-0036-9 • $16.99

Sound Design, Mixing, and Mastering with Ableton Live
by Jake Perrine
Softcover w/DVD-ROM •
978-1-4584-0037-6 • $16.99

The Power in Reason
by Andrew Eisele
Softcover w/DVD-ROM •
978-1-4584-0228-8 • $16.99

Sound Design and Mixing in Reason
by Andrew Eisele
Softcover w/DVD-ROM •
978-1-4584-0229-5 • $16.99

Mixing and Mastering with Pro Tools
by Glenn Lorbecki
Softcover w/DVD-ROM •
978-1-4584-0033-8 •$16.99

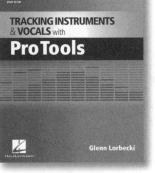

Tracking Instruments and Vocals with Pro Tools
by Glenn Lorbecki
Softcover w/DVD-ROM •
978-1-4584-0034-5 •$16.99

The Power in Logic Pro: Songwriting, Composing, Remixing, and Making Beats
by Dot Bustelo
Softcover w/DVD-ROM •
78-1-4584-1419-9 • $16.99

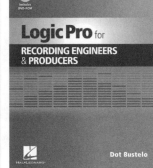

Logic Pro for Recording Engineers and Producers
by Dot Bustelo
Softcover w/DVD-ROM •
978-1-4584-1420-5 • $16.99

The Power in Cubase: Tracking Audio, MIDI, and Virtual Instruments
by Matthew Loel T. Hepworth
Softcover w/DVD-ROM • 978-1-4584-1366-6 • $16.99

Mixing and Mastering with Cubase
by Matthew Loel T. Hepworth
Softcover w/DVD-ROM • 978-1-4584-1367-3 • $16.99

Prices, contents, and availability subject to change without notice.

0312